SPELL
CRAFTS

About the Authors

Scott Cunningham practiced elemental magic for more than twenty years. He was the author of more than thirty books, both fiction and nonfiction. Cunningham's books reflect a broad range of interests within the New Age sphere, where he was highly regarded. He passed from this life on March 28, 1993, after a long illness.

David Harrington lives in Chula Vista, California, and has a long-time interest in the mysteries of magic. *Spell Crafts* is the second book on which he collaborated with Scott Cunningham, who was his teacher and friend.

SPELL CRAFTS

CREATING

MAGICAL

OBJECTS

SCOTT CUNNINGHAM
& DAVID HARRINGTON

2003
Llewellyn Publications
St. Paul, MN 55164-0383, U.S.A.

SECOND EDITION
First printing, 2003
FIRST EDITION, ten printings

Book design and editing by Kimberly Nightingale
Cover design by Kevin R. Brown
Cover painting 2002 © Anthony Meadows
Interior illustrations by Tom Clifton

Library of Congress Cataloging-in-Publication Data
Cunningham, Scott, 1956–1993
Spell crafts : creating magical objects / Scott Cunningham & David Harrington.
p.   cm. — (llewellyn's practical magic series)
Includes bibliographical references.
ISBN 0-87542-185-7
1. Handicraft. 2. Magic. I. Harrington, David. II. Title. III. Series.
TT157.C78   1993   93-24190
133.4'4—dc20   CIP

Llewellyn Worldwide does not participate in, endorse, or have any authority or responsibility concerning private business transactions between our authors and the public.
  All mail addressed to the author is forwarded but the publisher cannot, unless specifically instructed by the author, give out an address or phone number.
  Any Internet references contained in this work are current at publication time, but the publisher cannot guarantee that a specific location will continue to be maintained. Please refer to the publisher's website for links to authors' websites and other sources.

The old-fashioned remedies in this book are historical references used for teaching purposes only. The recipes are not for commercial use or profit. The contents are not meant to diagnose, treat, prescribe, or substitute consultation with a licensed healthcare professional.

Llewellyn Publications
A Division of Llewellyn Worldwide, Ltd.
P.O. Box 64383, Dept. 0-87542-185-7
St. Paul, MN 55164-0383, U.S.A.
www.llewellyn.com

Printed in the United States of America

Other Books by the Authors

The Magical Household

Other Books by Scott Cunningham

The Complete Book of Incense, Oils & Brews
Cunningham's Encyclopedia of Crystal, Gem & Metal Magic
Cunningham's Encyclopedia of Magical Herbs
Dreaming the Divine
Earth, Air, Fire & Water
Earth Power
Hawaiian Magic & Spirituality
Living Wicca
Magical Aromatherapy
The Truth About Herb Magic
The Truth About Witchcraft Today
Wicca

Biography of Scott Cunningham

Whispers of the Moon
(*written by David Harrington and deTraci Regula*)

Video of Scott Cunningham

Herb Magic

This book is dedicated to those who, in the distant past,
first revealed these techniques to their human worshippers.

Acknowledgments

To Nana Hughs for technical assistance; to Hazel Cunningham for providing wheat weaving information; to Dorothy for giving Scott his first magical craft lessons, and for our friends who have put up with us for five years while we wrote this book. To all of the above-named, our sincerest gratitude.

Table of Contents

part three: the tables

PREFACE TO THE SECOND EDITION

DURING THE WRITING of *The Magical Household*, Scott Cunningham and I looked at each other one day and realized that while describing the magic of the home for our readers was enjoyable, it would be still more fun to actually help furnish the reader's magical household. I would grow tired of research and put together craft projects for us to do as a break from the research and writing, so *The Magical Household* was written on tables overflowing with bits of yarn, broomstraw, beads, and other items. It seemed like it was the perfect time to start sharing these practical projects with others, and so *Spell Crafts* was born.

I had always enjoyed crafts, and when I became involved in magic, it seemed natural to incorporate the two together as often as possible. Scott and I were both ardent collectors of magical folk art, often visiting Mexico to buy native corn dollies, Day of the Dead statuary, and other local treasures. One of my favorites remain the Huichol "ojos de dios" or "eyes of God" made of yarn and sticks, which we also incorporated into the "Shaman's Arrow" project. It is simple enough to make, if you know the secret, which we share here.

I still enjoy referring to the "Magic of the Hands" chapter myself. This section was written by Scott and I think it is the most eloquent description he ever did of the process of magical empowerment. As humans, our hands set us apart from any other creature on earth, and anything we make with our hands is empowered with our own natural magic. When a craft is created with magical intent, the result is a beautiful, potent object that is a pleasure to see and to use.

It's marvelous to me that *Spell Crafts* has found such a large audience over the ten years it has been in print. Scott would be pleased with the enduring success of this project that was such a pleasure to create. I'm very glad to present this new edition and hope it will introduce many more people to the joy of making magic with your own hands.

David Harrington
Chula Vista, California
January 5, 2002

PREFACE

WHILE DAVID HARRINGTON and I were working on what was to become *The Magical Household*, we began discussing our next project. Given our interest in handicrafts, we decided that it would be focused on the creation of unusual magical objects—*a magical craft book*, we'd tell each other.

The Magical Household was published in 1987. We immediately began work on the next project, little realizing the challenges that faced us. Conflicting schedules, my continuous labors on other books, and the unusual nature of this topic kept us from completing it in a timely manner.

We persevered. Though none of the crafts described in this book were new to us, we began using them in new and different ways. We also had to determine the best method of writing down what are, at times, rather complicated instructions. This necessitated a great deal of practical experimentation.

We wove wheat, dipped candles, sculpted clay, tied god's eyes, mixed herbs, beaded sacred symbols, and fashioned spell brooms. Once we'd perfected these varieties of spell crafts, we began writing. Research provided clues as to the origins of some of these arts and this, too, became part of the book.

Five years later, we've finished *Spell Crafts*. In a magical sense, the creation of this book was also a form of spell craft. We had a goal: to write this book. We took raw materials (our ideas and experiences) and transformed them into a new form (the book) with our energies and hands. Our visualizations of the completed book have been manifested.

We freely admit that this is an unusual book. It challenges the reader to take part in the entire magical process, from crafting the tools to utilizing them in ritual. It hearkens back to the days when everything was handmade, when stores were few and people had to be self-reliant.

Spell Crafts presents powerful tools of positive self-transformation. None of them, however, can be effective unless they're actually made and used. Many of us feel the urge to create with magic, we can use that urge to improve the quality of our lives, and that makes the time and energy involved well worthwhile.

Welcome to the *true* craft of magic.

Scott Cunningham
La Mesa, California
June 24, 1992

INTRODUCTION

THERE ARE MANY types of magical tools. This book doesn't include instructions for the crafting of knives and swords, censers, wands, and other tools of ritual magic. We wish to make that clear right from the beginning.

It is, however, a guide to the creation and use of magical objects of a different nature. It's a book of craft merged with magic; of works of the mind and hand as well as of power. Within its pages lie instructions for creating a wide variety of unusual magical objects for an array of purposes—together with their ritual uses.

Magicians have always known that tools crafted with their own hands are more powerful than those made by others. During the creation process, specific energy can be placed within the object to enhance its effectiveness. This is the essence of spell craft: creating and empowering objects during their construction (or directly afterward) for a specific magical purpose.

Magic is no great mystery save to those who have never investigated or practiced it. It's the natural process of moving energy from within ourselves (or within natural objects) to create positive change. In spell craft, some of these changes are physical (clay is shaped; yarn is wrapped; herbs are mixed). Other changes are internal (personal power is directed toward a goal) and external (the magic's goal is manifested in the magician's life).

Spell craft may seem to be a new idea, but it's as old as the day when a human first shaped a natural object to fulfill a spiritual need. The timeless magic that we've presented here still speaks to our kind. It calls to the innate human urge to create. Spell craft nurtures our need to shape natural materials as well as our lives into new and pleasing forms. It also links us with our ancestors, who lived in a far smaller, less complex world of forms and energies.

In taking up these spell crafts today, we can use the techniques of earlier times to bring order and happiness into our lives.

Spell craft is, therefore, unique. Still, it's as old as the hills, the stars, and the moon. The rhythms of crafters echo those of the universe and the multitude of cycles that swirl around us.

May all your crafts be magical.

part one
beginnings

CHAPTER ONE

The Magic of Hands

HANDS WERE THE first magical tools. Long before the earliest spell books were written, humans saw their hands as tools of power. With them they changed their world, and change is the essence of magic.

In the earliest days of our species,* hands were used to gather and to prepare food, to create shelter, for making simple garments, and to fashion tools of wood, bone, stone, and shell. Hands clasped together during the beginnings of life, assisted during birth, struck against flesh in combat, and laid the deceased to rest. Finally, humans discovered they could use their hands to create fire. These quite real changes were probably viewed as the products of what we would term magic, for many of them were the sole province of humans.

---

* We can only speculate concerning the earliest spiritual and magical beliefs and practices, for there certainly are no written records. Speculation is based on a study of symbolism and a comparison with early historic civilizations, as well as with pretechnological peoples of more recent times.

Hands had other uses as well. Though some now speculate that early humans first communicated by telepathy, it seems possible that hand signals were also used. Apart from their value in everyday life (warning of danger, giving directions during hunts, passing on rudimentary knowledge), the language of gestures probably evolved specific signs reserved for religious and magical purposes. Certain shapes created with the fingers may have promoted union with spirit. Some were most probably magical in nature.

Thousands of years later, some of these early forms of communication were specifically associated with religion. Some of these ritual gestures have been preserved and are still used in religions found throughout the world*.

The miraculous changes that could be created with hands drove humans to regard them as one of the most spiritual parts of the body. In the first great civilizations (Sumer, Egypt, Greece, and Rome), hands enjoyed both a secular and a sacred aura of power, and played important roles in religion.

Sumerian images of worshippers were often carved with their hands held upward in supplication or clasped in humility. Wall paintings in Egyptian tombs depict deities holding ankhs—symbols of life—in their hands. In reliefs of Ra (an Egyptian sun deity), the rays stemming from the solar orb terminate in small hands.

Pagan deities from around the world are often depicted holding or clutching symbols of their powers (which are dispensed through their hands). Some Hindu deities are equipped with multiple arms and hands to symbolize the many powers and influences that these deities possess.

Even while hands were being used in religious capacities, they never lost their magical qualities. Hand-to-hand combat fostered the idea that hands were protective. Eventually, hands created symbols in their own images. Figures of hands were painted or carved and worn for protective purposes in ancient Egypt, Greece,

---

*All scuba divers are aware of the importance of gestures as a means of communication.

Rome, Asia, and possibly South America. The powers of hands were transferred from flesh to bronze, stone, wood, clay, silver, and gold. For example, protective door knockers from ancient Pompeii were fashioned in the form of a hand grasping a ball. (Representations of hands are still worn today throughout the Middle East, Europe, and Latin America, as they have been since ancient Greek times.)

As systems of magic evolved, hands became increasingly important: specific figures were drawn or traced, the hands were placed in certain postures, and ritual tools were carried and moved. Though many inner processes were at work during magical rituals, hands were viewed as the channels through which magical energy was released.

Even today, hands haven't lost their power. "Laying on of hands" is a popular form of healing, in which the hands are used to transport energy into the sick. The age-old art of palmistry hasn't died out. Gestures of love (holding hands) and hate (in the United States, the upraised middle finger) still evoke powerful emotions.

To symbolize the depth of our sincerity while swearing oaths, we raise a hand. Clasping hands upon meeting a friend is a social ritual in the West today, and is a survivor of the ancient ritual demonstration of exhibiting weapon-free hands (and thus, of friendly intentions).

We still wear betrothal, healing, and luck rings on our fingers, perhaps with the unconscious hope that placing such special objects on our fingers will strengthen their effectiveness. Some of us shake hands with famous persons, hoping that "luck" will rub off. Business transactions are often sealed with a ritual handshake. Semisecret groups continue to utilize ritual handclaspings as a means of recognition, and, throughout the world, most of us earn our living by using our hands.

Religious use of the hands is also with us. Catholics trace the sign of the cross on their bodies during prayer, priests and ministers often lift a hand during prayer and supplication (as religious persons have been doing since ancient Sumer), and Asians clap before images of their deities during religious ritual.

The wide range of unusual rituals and customs that we still perform with our hands hints at the magical potential contained within them. Our hands are far more than utilitarian objects: our palms and fingers are potent magical tools. Even several millennia of cultural and technological progress hasn't been able to fully exorcise this knowledge, as demonstrated by the above four paragraphs. Knowingly or unknowingly, we still affirm that hands are magical objects.

Magicians (those conversant with natural but little understood transformative techniques) know that the human body produces energy that can be used in magic. The hands are seen as conduits through which this energy is sent from the body during magical rites.

And so, hands are truly magical tools. With their help we can change our lives. Any creative act performed with the hands (writing a letter, weaving a rug, building a house, or knitting a sweater) can be an act of magic, if it's done with the proper intent.

So, what, exactly, is magic? We discuss this subject at length in chapter 3, but a few words are appropriate here. Magic is the movement of natural (yet subtle) energies to create positive change. It's an ancient art, rich with centuries of history and practice. It isn't supernatural, evil, or dangerous.

Many have found magic to be a technique that allows them to gain control over their lives; to transform them into happier, more positive experiences.

Spell craft is a special category of magic. It consists of the magical creation of, and ritual use of, magical objects. When we make such objects, we're performing acts of magic, for we're causing transformations (the raw materials and energies within them) with our hands.

Magic can be a purely mental process, using no tools other than a trained mind. More often, though, it involves the use of specific objects as focal points for concentration, such as candles, brooms, and herbs. These objects are usually handled in ritual ways while energy from within the body is sent into or through them.

This book describes many of these tools. Such objects, specifically made for a specific magical act, can be quite effective. The tools described in this book are rarely available in stores, but you can make them—with your hands.

All hand-made objects contain a bit of energy. The process that creates these objects is more than a simple repetition of techniques. During the creation process the craftsperson, through concentration and the physical activity involved, moves energy from within the body, through the hands, and into the material being worked. This is what sets it apart from other objects, and what readies it for use in magic.

In magic, we have the opportunity to imbue our crafts with specific energies: a loving relationship, increased money, protection against harm, enhanced spirituality, a sense of peace, physical and emotional purification, and psychic awareness. Today, many are seeking the spiritual dimension of our physical world. Though some of us enjoy the increasingly complex manifestations of applied technology, we're also searching for subtle explanations of the ways in which we interact with nature.

We're also eager to take control of our lives, to fill them with positive energy, to wash them clean of doubt, guilt, depression, poverty, and pain. Magic is a tool that can be used to do this, and the magic starts in our own hands.

The aim of magic isn't the domination of nature; it's the domination of ourselves. We can clasp magic as a tool of positive self-transformation. Spell craft is one aspect of this tool. Sewing beads, weaving wheat, and creating magical brooms affirms, through simple techniques and rituals, the powers within our hands and their ability to shape our lives into nurturing, evolving experiences.

Look at your hands as they really are. See them as wondrous vehicles of power, of the energy that flows through everything you do. Tap into that power! Carve a symbol, dip a candle, mix fragrant herbs, sculpt clay, and make your life all that you want it to be.

Create objects of magic and use them to transform your life into a positive experience. In doing so you'll celebrate nature, your hands and, ultimately, yourself.

CHAPTER TWO

The True Meaning of Craft

THE WORD "CRAFT" has today acquired a mundane definition. A craft is a manual art, usually indulged in for enjoyment (and, occasionally, for monetary reward). Some crafts are also seen as arts; thus, they can be viewed as mediums of personal expression. The Industrial Revolution, which negated the need for many hand-made articles, also revolutionized our attitudes toward crafts.

Crafts have largely become pastimes, often associated with the very young, the elderly, or with emotionally and intellectually challenged persons (the popular concept of therapy as "basket-weaving" is an excellent example of the latter).

Craft was once seen in its proper perspective, however. Indigenous cultures throughout the world have always claimed that crafts were of divine revelation, not human invention. Pottery, beading, painting, agriculture, medicine, spinning, weaving, knotting, brewing, carving—these were techniques that had been created by the goddesses and gods, the spirits, the divine ones.

All crafts were intimately linked with spirituality. A woman who carefully shaped a water jar from clay she'd gathered from a river bank was performing a spiritual practice, and was fully aware of this fact.

When crafts were used to create objects intended for ritual, or that symbolized the divine, the connection between the craftsperson and divinity grew more intense: the revealed techniques would be used to exalt their revealers.

Since all crafts were sacred, the craftspersons practicing them weren't simply transforming objects. Working the craft was a rite of spiritual connection between the worker and the deity. Thus, craft was never simply a pastime: it was a rite of power and honor; a religious ritual.

Craftspersons may have also been aware of the dual nature of craft. Outwardly, the craftsperson transformed raw materials into new forms and structures. Inwardly, the material also transformed the craftsperson. Thus, each craft was also a spiritually evolving process that created both physical and nonphysical change.

In the earliest times of our species, religion and magic were identical. Little distinction could be made between praying to the sun as it rose and carrying an etched stone as protection against the warriors from the neighboring village. Both actions were connected with nonphysical, abstract aspects of human life, both were little understood, and both were of vital importance to their practitioners.

Many examples of what seem to be magical and/or religious pieces have been discovered in prehistoric European grave sites. The fact that such objects were made, rather than found, probably lent them additional power and effectiveness, for the techniques used to create them were divinely revealed. This linked them with the unfathomable powers of the sky, sun, wind, lightning, and the earth itself.

Nearer historical times, magical objects were made of every available material (wood, shell, stone, clay, bone, feathers, skin, fur, flowers, seeds). Most of these seem to have been created for protective purposes. At times, the material itself wasn't important. Of greater significance was the fact that the craftsperson had molded and shaped it to suit her or his needs. This object, once made and properly used, assisted the person in molding and shaping her or his life as well.

Before the invention of the assembly line; before Christian dominance in the western world, craft was a spiritual/magical art, a practice of power, of inward and outward control. We retain just a hint of this original meaning in the word "Witchcraft," which refers to the "craft" of the "Witch." Only Witches and magicians managed to retain the magical knowledge of craft. The craft of the Witch consisted of many things, including magic, herbal medicine, the use of psychic awareness, midwifery, counseling, and weather prediction, as well as the creation of magical physical objects.

Many early Witches, when asked, made charms, mixed medicinal brews, and fashioned protective amulets for those that came to them for help. The traditional Witch was intimately familiar with the energies inherent in craft itself.

Though the spiritual/magical nature of crafts was largely forgotten, the crafts themselves were kept alive. The Middle Ages and the Renaissance did much to funnel crafts into purely Christian channels. Certain crafts (including masonry, carpentry, and lapidary) were related to the glorification of "God"; other, homelier crafts lost all spiritual significance and became mere occupations.

The word "Witch" soon instilled fear, not necessarily of the Witches themselves, but of the power of a religion that viciously used this term to eliminate its enemies. The craft of the Witch soon inspired dread. Crafts in any way linked with magic could prompt arrests, trials, and executions. Witches and their crafts drew back into the shadows, taking with them the few remaining vestiges of the true meaning of craft.

The nature of craft was slowly changing. Craft lost much of its spiritual meaning (except within the church's definition) and the old art of crafting charms and amulets were either altered to quasi-Christian forms or were altogether forgotten. Craft became a mundane pursuit whose practitioners thought no further than producing the goods in question (many of which were, admittedly, things of beauty). Magical objects were only created in private and used in complete secrecy. Our understanding of craft had changed.

If we're to truly use craft as a tool of magic, we must become aware of its larger purpose. Craft consists of more than the mere slapping together of clay or the dipping of candles. Craft is a transformative process that we can use to change both ourselves and our lives.

Many of the techniques that we've outlined in this book may seem to be rather mundane, in spite of the objects created with them. This isn't the case. Each aspect of every craft is in itself an act of magic. From gathering the materials to empowering and utilizing the finished project, each step is a vital part of the craft's magic.

Craft, then, is more than a manual art. It's a connection with ourselves; a valuable tool that we can use to alter our lives. The art of craft is one that can be mastered by anyone with a willingness to learn and a deep desire for self-transformation. This can be achieved only with a clear understanding of the true meaning of craft.

CHAPTER THREE

What Is Magic?

THIS BOOK DISCUSSES the creation and use of magical objects. You needn't undergo lengthy magical studies to successfully use this information. Becoming familiar with some basic magical techniques, however, will ensure better results.

This chapter is an overview of magic. If you're an experienced folk magician, consider it as a review. If not, then look upon this chapter as an introduction to a brand new world.

What Magic Is and Isn't

Magic is the movement of natural energies to create needed change. Magic isn't a supernatural process; it simply uses energies that haven't yet been fully explained—even by magicians themselves. (Many mysteries still exist, both within and outside of magic. Pick up any issue of *Scientific American* and you'll see the truth of this statement.)

Magic isn't a practice that uses powers derived from the "Devil." It isn't antireligious or anti-God; it's simply nonreligious (though it can be used in religious ways).

Magic isn't a weapon. Magic isn't a supernatural tool to be unleashed against those we dislike. It isn't an instrument of manipulation, destruction, or death. Misuse of magic destroys its misuser.

If there is one universal rule among magicians, it is this: harm none.

The Goal of Magic

As described above, magic is utilized to bring about needed change. The needed change is often termed the goal. This goal may involve love, protection, health, peace, prosperity, increased spirituality, psychic awareness, or other changes. The goal of magical rites should always be positive.

From a broader perspective, the ultimate goal of all magic is the improvement of our lives. We can create this improvement through the use of magic. We decide what's best for us, and magic is a tool that we can use to obtain it.

Working Magic for Others

Magicians aren't selfish. They utilize magic to improve their lives, yes, but they also help others who come to them with problems. Before performing magical acts for other persons, inform them of your intentions, and receive permission for the working. If you're making a magically charged object for a friend, ask before creating it if such an object would be accepted. Such measures will ensure that you're not influencing and altering others' lives without their consent.

Magical Energy

The energy used in magic is natural. It's present within our bodies as well as in physical objects such as sand, wood, stone, clay, fire, air, feathers, and every other part of the earth.

Magic is simply the use of these powers. It seems mysterious today only because most of its techniques have been forgotten.

Some people claim to have magical powers. I certainly hope they don't consider themselves to be anything special. We all possess this power, and we can learn how to use it. All that's required is an open mind and a willingness to practice.

The Three Types of Magical Energy

Personal power is that which resides within us. This is the energy that we use in our daily lives; that empowers our thought processes and keeps our "souls" attached to flesh and blood.

We're born with some of this energy, that which is passed to us from our biological mothers and fathers. Though we expend *personal power* every day, we also absorb it in the form of food, sunlight, water, air, and the emotions (such as love and concern) that are directed toward us by our friends and family.

When we exercise, run for the phone, become nervous or angry, pedal a bicycle, or simply breathe, we expend personal power. This is why extended physical effort creates exhaustion, for we're literally drained of energy.

Magicians also expend personal power, but they do so for the specific purpose of creating a needed change. This is achieved through certain techniques that are discussed later in this chapter. The power sent forth from the body is the same as that released by an athlete, but the magician molds and shapes it so that it can be of specific use in achieving a goal.

Personal power is allowing you to read this book, turn the pages, and concentrate on its information. If you're eating while reading these words, you're replenishing your store of personal power. Nothing is more natural than personal power.

Earth power consists of the manifestations of energy around us; the products of the earth as well as our planet itself. Think of the earth as a lens that transforms nonphysical energy into specific physical forms such as plants, water, stones, sand, and so on.

Each specific type of natural object possesses its own range of energies. A sunflower, for instance, has far different energies than a lump of clay. All the things on the earth—animate or inanimate; animal, vegetable, or mineral; gaseous, liquid, or solid—possess a special and unique form of earth power.

Thousands of plants and stones (the two manifestations of earth power most commonly used in magic) have been placed into specific classifications of magical use. In other words, magicians have found that a certain stone works well in attracting love, a certain plant for speeding the healing of the human body, a certain flower for expanding love. Matching such "forms" (natural objects) to the nature of the goal is one aspect of the magical art.

Spell craft utilizes personal power with earth power. While working with shells, stones, herbs, and wheat, we're mixing our energies with the energies of these substances and molding them into magical objects. The combination of personal power with earth power is far stronger and more effective than is personal power alone.

Divine power doesn't usually exist on the earth. It's nonphysical, eternal, omnipotent. Divine power is the power that created the universe.

Though magic isn't a religious practice, some magicians do indeed invoke divine power to assist them in their magical workings: the Goddess and/or God is asked to bless the ritual and to send energy to enhance its effects. This certainly isn't always the case. Still, those magicians who have established links with deity can bring religion into their craft work. This is a matter of personal choice.

Spells and Rituals

A spell or ritual consists of a specific series of actions, words, and other events that end in the movement of energy. In magic, the two words are interchangeable (though in religion, rituals are spiritual expressions of faith—not magical actions).

There are many types of rituals. We perform some rituals every day. We may sit down to dinner at a certain time, read the paper in the morning, put on one shoe before donning the other. These rituals produce needed change: they feed us, inform us, and protect our feet. These are personal rituals.

In this country, we drive on the right side of the road, wait for a table in a restaurant, pass persons walking toward us on the right, and shake hands or hug upon meeting a friend. Doing these things ensures that we drive safely, won't be thrown out of a restaurant, won't bump into others, and that we acknowledge the presence of someone we know. These are social rituals.

In attending religious services, we may wear special clothing or headgear, speak in unusual languages, pray in unison, sing specific songs, and do many other things. Performing such actions enriches our spiritual experience.

These are religious rituals. We might also set a specific goal in our minds, take up needle and thread, and create a craft. Or we may light a candle and say a short chant. We do these things to create a positive change in our lives. These are magical rituals.

Ritual is nothing new: we're performing rituals every day of our lives. Magical ritual is simply a different type of ritual, but it's as real and as effective as any of the other types discussed above, and produces just as specific effects.

Magical rituals are sometimes dramatic representations of our magical goal. They may also be quite subtle. They have three purposes: to put us into the proper frame of mind, and to allow us to combine personal power with earth power, and, eventually, to send that power to do its task.

Old spells aren't necessarily more effective than new ones. Published rituals don't tend to be ineffective simply because they've been published. All properly designed spells will work if they're properly performed.

In magic, the world of energies is just as real as that of kittens, bills, and rainbows. Spells and rituals allow us to penetrate the illusion that the physical world is the ultimate reality; that our lives are predetermined; that we have no control over them. They give us control.

Magical Visualization

This consists of the practice of creating images of your goal in the mind. In magic, the mind is recognized as a powerful tool in shaping and forming energy. Positive thinking is an example of this, but magicians take this one step further. They use the mind's creative abilities to produce three-dimensional pictures of the magical goal.

In other words, a magician suffering from a lack of money to pay bills might form a mental image of her or himself paying the bills. She or he might then use this visualization to "program" personal power and earth power with money-attracting energies. Visualization gives the power its purpose.

This needn't seem so mysterious. Most of us visualize every day. We imagine ourselves driving a dream car, or walking into our new home at the edge of the forest beside a trickling stream. We recall the faces of physically distant friends, or remember the sights of our last vacation.

Magical visualization is simply an extension of this. Rather than recalling the past, we create images of things that we haven't yet seen or experienced.

Many excellent guides to creative visualization exist, but here are a few pointers. To successfully visualize, it's necessary to allow yourself to do so. Everyone, to some degree, can visualize. Don't try too hard. Don't push yourself. Relax and do it.

Sit quietly with your eyes closed. Choose one of the following scenes or objects to visualize (but don't visualize other persons). Make the mental image as real as possible in your mind. Remember: choose one image and use it exclusively.

- See the front door of your home— or the condition of your kitchen sink.
- See your favorite article of clothing.
- See your favorite pet.
- See your favorite food.
- See your favorite flower.

Practice this for at least a few minutes a day for a week. Once you're confident that you're able to create this image, you're ready to move to the next step.

This consists of broadening the scope of your visualization. Choose one of the following, or create your own. Visualize your favorite food, but taste it as well. Visualize your favorite perfume or flower, and smell it as well. Visualize a band, rock group, symphony orchestra, or a bell, and hear it as well. Visualize a large block of ice—and feel its chill in your hands. Continue this for a week. (Though you won't have to always smell or hear your visualizations, this exercise will strengthen your overall visualization abilities.)

Next, pick a goal. This could be getting out of debt, finding a love, working at a more satisfying job, passing a test with confidence. Choose a plausible goal.

Visualize yourself attaining this goal. (If you've forgotten how you look, peek into a mirror; it's often necessary to visualize yourself.) Using the skills that you've developed from the above exercises, see yourself paying those bills, meeting that person, working at that better job, passing that test. Make this image as real as is possible. Know that this change is about to occur.

When you can do this, when you can create such a visualization and know that it's real, you're ready to work magic.

Rousing, Programming, Releasing, and Directing Energy

This is the heart of magic. Without using this four-fold process, incantations are useless and rituals are ineffective. They're necessary for the empowerment of magical objects. Here are the four processes. *Rousing* consists of awakening personal power and earth power. *Programming* is the process of infusing this power with a specific magical goal through visualization. *Releasing* is the act of moving the energy from within our bodies. *Directing* consists of aiming the roused, programmed, and released power into a specific object. (This process may begin as you begin the craft. Alternately, it may be done after the craft has been completed.)

Empowerment as You Begin

Every project contained within this book is related to a specific goal. Once you've chosen an appropriate project and have gathered the needed supplies, it's time to begin.

Visualize your goal. Fix this image in your mind. Pour all your concentration and emotion into the goal. As you do this, touch the objects that you'll be using. Program them with energy and begin to work the craft. Feel your muscles flexing as you work. Realize that they're releasing energy into the object on which you're working. Channel the programmed energy into the object. Continue the visualization for as long as possible.

Empowerment After Completion

If the object is empowered after its completion, a slightly different process is used. Visualize and empower the objects that you'll be using. When the project has been completed, stand before it and build power within you by tightening the muscles in your body. Intensify your visualization. Hold the power inside you. When you can wait no longer, push the power out from your body through your hand. Feel it racing down your arm and out of your fingers. Simultaneously, direct the power through your fingers and into the object. Send it in a straight line into the craft. Don't just give it directions—send it there. Empowering a craft is, after all, an act of power. This aspect of magic isn't a walk in the country; it's work. (Immediately after releasing the energy, relax for a few moments.)

That's it. The energy has left you and entered the magical object, rousing and programming the object's energies and aligning them with your magical goal.

Once the object has been empowered, it's ready for use. The objects described in this book are used in many different ways, and no summary of them can be made here. Simply follow the instructions for each project.

Pointers for Directing Power

There are many different ways of directing the power. The hands are probably the most commonly used, for they're usually considered to be points at which personal power is naturally projected from the body. For right-handed persons, the right hand is the power-sending hand, simply because it's the most talented. Left-handed persons usually use the left hand. Ambidextrous folks can use either one.

Though you could use your eyelids or your elbows as power directors, the hands are the traditional avenues through which power is released. Always using the same hand to release energy (or even both hands) is best, for it'll soon become second nature.

The amount of energy released during magic isn't so great that it'll threaten your health, but you may feel both exhilarated and drained after such a ritual. If so, have a snack after the ritual. Drink a bit of water or fruit juice and eat something rich in protein. If you're in ill-health, it's best to wait to perform any works of magic other than those of self-healing.

If all this sounds mysterious, relax. Driving (or using a microwave oven) was also mysterious until you became familiar with these tools.

Many variations of this four-step process exist, but most effective rituals contain them all. Throughout this book we may direct you to "empower the object" or "bless it" or "build power." When we do, you'll know the techniques. They're right here.

Clockwise Motion

At several points in this book you'll be directed to perform some action in a clockwise motion. This follows an age-old magical practice of moving with the sun.

Sundials were created in antiquity as a method of determining the hour of the day. This timepiece consists of a flat disc inscribed with numbers and a pointer rising directly from its center. On cloudless, clear days, the pointer casts a shadow onto the numbers, and this determines the approximate hour.

As the hours of daylight progress, this shadow moves "clockwise," i.e., from the right to the left on the dish. For this and other reasons, earlier magicians deemed that this was an appropriate ritual direction for positive magic. It's easy to determine how to perform clockwise motions. While this may seem to be a simple matter, many are confused about it, and so a few words here are appropriate.

Cut a piece of paper into a rough circle. Mark the top of this circle *North*, the right *East*, the bottom *South*, and the left *West*. Move a finger from north to east to south to west. This is clockwise motion. (Moving your whole body clockwise is exactly the same: move from north to east to south to west.)

Clockwise motions are traditional—in this hemisphere. Below the equator, many magicians use counterclockwise motions. If you live there, you may wish to try this alternative.

Collection Rituals

During the course of this book you'll be asked to gather a forked branch, sand, or flowers. You might think, "Okay. I'll just get the chainsaw . . ."

This isn't the best approach. The earth and its resources are manifestations of divine energy, so we collect such objects with a reverent attitude of thankfulness. This isn't religion, it's spirituality, which we define as an awareness of something higher than ourselves.

Magicians certainly don't seek to destroy nature. Still, they realize that it's occasionally necessary to take from her storehouse. When this is so, they give something back.

One of the ways to achieve this is by using a collection ritual. We're presenting a few of our own below. You can either perform these or use them to create your own versions. Either way, it's best to perform some sort of ritual. (Collection rituals aren't necessary for purchased objects, unless you dare to buy fur or feathers.)

When scooping, plucking, or cutting, do so with peace. Do so with a sense of the interconnectedness of all things; with the awareness that the energies within natural objects are similar to those that empower our bodies. As you actually collect, say one of the following chants, or similar words.

A general collection chant:

> Earth of the green field;
> of sand, tree, and flower;
> I ask of your yield
> to lend me your power.

Another general collection chant:

> I take only what I give
> I take only what I need
> I take only what I'll use.

When collecting wood:

> O great tree; O strong tree,
> bring my magic goal to me.

If all else fails you simply say: "Thank you." (Many other chants can be created along these lines.)

It's also traditional to leave something behind at the collection site. This is a form of payment (energy exchange) for the precious object that you've taken. A few drops of honey, a stone, a coin, or a bit of silver or gold are traditional examples. Collect with reverence.

Having a Magical Attitude

This is a book of spell craft; a guide to creating physical objects for specific magical goals. It's far different from the magic books that contain directions for the utilization of purchased magical tools.

You're performing a magical ritual when engaged in any aspect of spell craft. From the collection of the needed items, to crafting, to the final shaping, charging, and use—these are all pieces of the magical puzzle. When they're fitted together, the object can perform its magical function.

View every step of your project as a part of a ritual. Give your whole attention to the project. Dipping spell candles while watching television will lessen the tapers' magical effectiveness. Give your entire attention to the project.

These works are meant to be fun, so you needn't be solemn about them. Simply direct your mind to your magical goal. Keep that visualization sharp and strong. In other words, create and maintain a magical attitude toward your craft, and your attention will be repaid.

Having a magical attitude contains these things, but it's far broader. It's also the knowledge that we can alter and transform our lives through the works of our own hands. It's the satisfaction of knowing that we no longer have to sit around and complain: we can do something about our problems.

It's also an awareness that the earth is a wondrous place of energy that deserves our respect.

These are some basics of magic. Practice rousing, programming, releasing, and directing energy. Sharpen the abilities of your hands to perform new, creative functions. Keep the goal of your magical ritual in mind throughout every session of spell craft.

And most of all, use spell craft as a means of improving your life and the lives of those you know and love.

CHAPTER FOUR

Empowering Your Crafts

WE PRESENT MANY magical crafts in this book. You needn't limit your spell crafting to those projects that we've included, however. All crafts have their magical origins, and can be used for magical purposes. This chapter examines some of the techniques that you can use to add a magic touch to the creation and the use of any type of craft.

One of the best methods that we've found to accomplish this is by following the plan below.

Determine Your Magical Need

Magic is never done for fun or to fulfill wishes. It's a serious practice used to satisfy your most basic needs. Determine your most pressing need. This will become your magical goal. (We use the words "goal" and "need" interchangeably in this book.)

Determine the Best Craft and Project to Fulfill this Need

The craft used and the project made may or may not be obviously and directly linked with the goal itself. However, it's certainly best if the created object can be utilized in some way. If you're a knitter, you could make a healing shawl or sweater. This would be an excellent use of this craft, for the sick person could wear the shawl, and thus directly absorb the healing energy. Use your imagination and craft experience.

If Possible, Use Only Natural Materials

Natural materials are the most potent, while synthetic materials contain no energy whatsoever. Synthetic cloth, nylon yarn, chemical glue, fake clay, plastic beads, and other artificial objects will harm the magical efficacy of any object in which they're used. Synthetics not only lack any power whatsoever, they're also quite ineffective in retaining power sent into them. They're simply not practical or effective magical tools and should be avoided at all costs. Nothing will hold power as efficiently as organic materials.

Design the project with its final magical use in mind. Though you could certainly sew a ritual toaster cover, it might be wiser to create something of more practical ritual use, such as a protective magic bag, a robe designed for ritual, love-drawing pajamas, or something a bit more useful. Of course, if you wished to bless your toast with specific energies each morning . . .

Gather Your Supplies with Your Goal in Mind

Once you've determined your magical goal, you're working to attain it. Gather the needed materials with visualization. See the completed project and its goal manifesting in your life.

Work on One Project at a Time

If you've been busily stitching a money rune on a green bag, don't suddenly switch to crafting a love potpourri. Concentrate your energies on a single project. Don't switch to another until you've completed the previous one. (It is fine, of course, to work on other, nonmagical crafts simultaneously with your magical project.)

Create Your Project with Ritual Intent

You may wish to simply visualize. Or, compose a short chant and say this while you're working. Your mind should be trained on both the physical and the magical aspects of the craft as you're working it. If necessary, plan time each day when you'll be alone and can work on the project without interruptions.

Send Energy into the Project during its Creation

This happens automatically, but your concentration and visualization will increase it.

Use the Completed Project

When you've completed and empowered the spell craft, use it in some appropriate ritual way. Light a candle, say a few words, perform some ritual motions. (Ideas can be gleaned from the examples included in this book).

Any craft can indeed be magical. Perfumes can be mixed with power. Magic words can be chanted while weaving. Beer can be brewed at specific times, with specific materials, with special powers. Household protectants can be woodburned, knives forged, and incense burners turned on a wheel.

A carpenter might create a "magic table," with a round top and runes carved into its legs, or a cabinet specially designed to house herbs and oils used in magic. A lapidary may create ritual jewelry, utilizing the proper stones and metals to bring specific influences into her or his life. The type of craft itself isn't as important as the purpose for which the object will be used.

So, though we've limited ourselves to a small number of specific types of craft in this book, all crafts can be practiced in ritual ways, and the fruits of these efforts can be utilized to create positive, needed changes in our lives.

part two
the ways

CHAPTER FIVE

Magical, Simmering Potpourri

As EARLY AS 1662, and perhaps long before that, herbs were deliberately simmered to produce pleasant fragrances in the home. This custom has continued to the present day in the form of the use of simmering potpourri.

Scent has an undeniable effect on humans. It can cheer us, calm us, promote hunger and thoughts of bygone days. Unexpectedly smelling a perfume or cologne may make us recall memories of loved ones.

Magicians have always known that scents can produce magical changes as well. Incense has long been smoldered to release energy during magical rites. Fragrant oils are still rubbed onto the body as part and parcel of a thousand-and-one spells. Aromatic herbs are also strewn, carried, brewed, or used in innumerable other magical ways.

Simmering potpourri are currently available in a wide variety of formulas. Fancy porcelain pots are also being marketed to be used with these mixtures. Unfortunately, nearly all potpourri mixtures offered for sale today receive little or no scent from true herbs, roots, seeds, and flowers. Many are composed of wood chips heavily doused with synthetic oils. A few dried flowers or spices may be added to improve the potpourri's visual appeal.

The ingredients of "strawberry" potpourri never grew in a field. Even such simple mixtures as lavender and rose usually have their origins far from the sun-drenched fields of France and Bulgaria. These potpourri have no magical effects, and often emit plasticky, vulgar scents.

It's possible, however, to use simmering potpourri in your home to effect magical changes. How? Simply make them yourself. The ingredients are generally inexpensive and readily available. (Those that can't be found at your local market can be ordered through the mail; see appendix.) The rituals used with these mixtures may seem simple, but the powers that waft through the house on the wings of scent are potent and cause both immediate and more long-lasting magical changes.

This chapter, then, is a guide to creating magical simmering potpourri. All that's needed is one pot (preferably nonmetallic), a stove, and the herbs themselves. While these mixtures can be used in commercially made "simmerers," these aren't necessary. We would, however, designate one pot for this purpose alone so that it's always available for use.

These mixtures make fine gifts if packed in canning jars, labeled, and tied with a ribbon of the appropriate color (see part 3).

The following recipes yield approximately enough for one use. These may be doubled or tripled and the magical potpourri kept in tight containers for later use.

To use these mixtures, fill a pot with at least two cups water. Add the mixture. Simmer over low heat for one-half hour or longer. If you'll be simmering for longer than a half hour, add more water. If you wish, use a potholder to carry the simmering pan around your house to further spread its energies. (A simmering potpourri pot can also be used.) As the scent rises, the power that you've placed into the potpourri is automatically released.

Never simmer such mixtures simply for fun, or to deodorize your home. To do so wastes their energies. Reserve your simmering potpourri for magical purposes and create general mixtures for deodorizing purposes.

Here's some of the magic of scent.

Love Simmering Potpourri

To expand, broaden, or to introduce love into your life, simmer this mixture of herbs. (This can also be used to strengthen a long-standing relationship, or to bring your own family closer together. Love begins within. Love yourself, then seek another with whom to share love.)

> 3 tablespoons rose petals
> 2 tablespoons camomile
> 1 tablespoon coriander
> 1 tablespoon lavender
> 1 teaspoon cinnamon
> ½ vanilla bean

Mix in a small bowl and charge with loving energies. Simmer while saying:

> *Love awakens*
> *in these rooms;*
> *come by the power*
> *of these blooms!*

Use every day.

Money Simmering Potpourri

If money is a problem rather than a pleasure, when you're faced with unexpected financial obligations, when the money you earn doesn't seem to come in fast enough, brew up one of these and set money-attracting energies into motion.

2 cinnamon sticks, broken into pieces
4 tablespoons whole cardamom seeds
2 tablespoons whole cloves
1 teaspoon ground nutmeg (or 2 whole nutmegs)
1 teaspoon ground ginger

With your fingers, mix these ingredients in a small bowl, while visualizing increased prosperity. As you mix them, say these or similar words:

Money simmer in the air;
money shimmer everywhere!

To use, simmer according to the instructions above.

Simmering potpourri

Protective Simmering Potpourri

Simmer this mixture at regular intervals (once a week or so) to drench your home with protective energy. This safeguards it from outside influences of all kinds—if it's performed with the proper intent.

> 4 tablespoons rosemary (whole)
> 3 bay leaves (whole)
> 1 tablespoon basil (whole)
> 1 tablespoon sage (whole)
> 1 tablespoon fennel (whole)
> 1 teaspoon dill seed (whole)
> 1 teaspoon juniper berries (whole)
> A pinch dried garlic (can be omitted)

Mix in small bowl with hands, visualizing your home as a protected place. Charge the herbs with protective energies. Add to simmering water.

When the scented steam rises, chant the following or similar words:

Air and water, work my will
to guard this house with power bold;
earth and fire, work to still
all dangers both untold and told.

Purification Simmering Potpourri

While spring cleaning or at any time you wish to clear away the cobwebs of useless energies that exist within all homes, after household arguments, when a roommate moves out, whenever tension is in the air, simmer this mixture with at least one window open. (During winter or rain, open the fireplace's damper, crack a window an inch, or otherwise ensure that there's a clear and easy path out of your home for the duration of the ritual.)

6 tablespoons peppermint
1 tablespoon spearmint
1 tablespoon rosemary
1 tablespoon dried lemon peel
1 tablespoon dried lime peel

Mix, charge, and simmer as you say these or similar words:

Scented breeze, blow pure and clear
unwanted power far from here.

Psychic Simmering Potpourri

If you wish to link your conscious mind with your psychic awareness, if you wish to use tarot cards or rune stones or other tools to glimpse possible future events, create this blend and simmer to stimulate your psychic mind.

3 tablespoons galangal
1 tablespoon star anise (or 2 whole)
1 tablespoon lemongrass
1 tablespoon thyme
1 tablespoon rose petals
A pinch mace
A pinch real saffron

Mix and charge the herbs in a small bowl. Visualize your psychic awareness as being under your control. Smell the fragrance rising from the herbs. Inhale the energies. Relax, chant the following words, and foretell.

Starlight swirls before my eyes;
twilight furls its wisdom wise;
moonlight curls within the skies:
the time has come to prophesize.

(We realize that genuine saffron, which is available at gourmet shops, is quite expensive. Just a pinch, however, is suggested here and it may be omitted.)

Magical Power Simmering Potpourri

To be used before and/or during all forms of magical rites. This formula boosts your reserve of personal power. Use at least four cups of water to simmer the following mixture.

> 4 tablespoons dried orange peel
> 4 tablespoons whole allspice
> 2 tablespoons ground ginger
> 2 whole carnations (preferably red)
>   or 1 tablespoon ground cloves

Charge the herbs and spices while mixing them in a small bowl. As you mix them, say these or similar words:

> *Flowers and spices*
> *charged by the sun*
> *help me ensure that*
> *magic is done.*
> *Open the path*
> *to my energy*
> *this is my will*
> *and so mote it be!*

Simmer and let the herbs' powers fill the air as you do your magical working. (Remember to turn off the stove after your ritual.)

CHAPTER SIX

A Psychic Mandala

FROM THE EARLIEST times, we've created forms of self-decoration. This is understandable. Early humans must have looked in wonder at the fantastic colors and patterns that decorated the creatures of the land, sea, and air. In contrast, humans must have seemed quite drab.

To compensate for this lack of natural ornamentation, our ancestors created the earliest forms of jewelry using bright feathers, shiny stones, unique shells, seed pods, even teeth and bones. Stringing such objects on tough grasses or on thin strips of animal hide, the first necklaces, belts, armlets, and anklets were created tens of thousands of years ago.

Many examples of such early forms of jewelry have been recovered at prehistoric archaeological sites. Seemingly mystical incisions found on some of these items, viewed in light of our knowledge of ritual jewelry use in later cultures, suggest that these necklaces and pendants were worn for more than bodily adornment. They were most certainly thought to imbue their wearers with the magical properties of the materials from which they were made. Even in this far distant time, jewelry was associated with magic.

Perhaps the earliest form of magical jewelry was found on the skull of the prehistoric Grimaldi man, which was carbon dated at approximately 90,000 B.C.E. Placed around the top of the skull was a circlet made from matching, small, round marine mollusks strung in a bead-like pattern. These were the forerunners of the perfect glass beads that weren't to be made for several millennia.

Today we know that these beads originated in ancient Meso-potamia, in the areas now occupied by Iran and Iraq. Smooth, highly polished carnelian beads were found on a necklace of *Dentalium* (tooth-shaped) shells dated to perhaps 5500 B.C.E. Additionally, archaeologists excavating the royal cemetery of Ur found exquisite beads of gold and precious stones. Beads made of such expensive materials must have been the sole property of royalty, and were often intimately related to specific deities. Beads were also used as amulets to drive away evil or talismans to attract specific, beneficial energies.

Soon, however, the masses were demanding their own beads. Faience (a form of self-glazing clay) was used to make less expensive beads. In Egypt, around 1500 B.C.E., glass was finally developed. This revolutionary process was soon used to create glass beads and imitation precious stones.

Ancient Egypt sent glass beads to the more "barbaric" peoples of Europe. Soon, this means of decoration became a medium of exchange and barter unhindered by local currency; hence the term "trade beads."

The first European bead factories were established in Venice and Murano, Italy. Mass-produced beads became widely available, and soon made their way to the United States.

Before the coming of the Europeans, American Indians fashioned beads from a variety of materials including bone, claw, and stone. Perhaps the most famous of these was wampum, which was made from clam, conch, and periwinkle shells. The word "wampum" originated in the Algonquin term *warn pum peak* or *wamponaqe*, meaning "string of beads."

Settlers and traders to North America brought beads with them. Eventually, the European glass beads all but replaced locally made beads. European glass beads were used as money, as well as for the decoration of clothing and ritual objects.

European explorers spread trade beads around the world. Soon, these small glass wonders, in various sizes and colors, replaced many other locally produced beads. Their shimmering appearance, wide range of colors, and easy availability ensured their universal acceptance, even in religious and magical applications.

Today, many beads are available for far less than a cent each. But they still haven't lost their aura of magic.

Beaded Psychic Mandala

We'll be making a beaded psychic mandala that utilizes form as well as color. It's designed to create psychic awareness within its wearer.

Items needed:

1 6-inch embroidery hoop
Purple felt
#0 beading needle (these are different than normal needles; they're longer, thinner, and have a smaller eye. Check at arts and crafts shops, variety stores, or the mail-order suppliers listed in the appendix.)
Purple or blue thread (any type can be used—experiment.)
Blue #10 gauge glass seed beads
Purple #10 gauge glass seed beads (see appendix)
Scissors
Household glue
A large, flat rock, ideally with a slanted side, upon which to place your finished project
A blue candle and candle holder

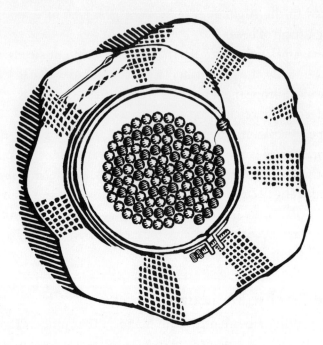

Beaded Psychic Mandala

Step 1. Assemble all items. Put felt onto embroidery hoop and secure. Thread needle, knot one end of thread, and push needle through center of felt from reverse side. Pull thread taut.

Step 2. Place one blue bead onto needle; sew tightly onto center of felt. This is the center bead—the middle of the project.

Step 3. Sew a purple bead beside the center blue bead. Position it as close to the center bead as possible. Sew purple beads in a circle around the center bead, once again closely positioning them. Make the beads touch each other.

Step 4. Sew a circle of blue beads around the purple circle.

Step 5. Sew a circle of purple beads.

Step 6. Sew a circle of blue beads.

Step 7. Sew a circle of purple beads.

Step 8. Sew a circle of blue beads.

Step 9. Sew a circle of purple beads.

Step 10. Sew a circle of blue beads. When you've sewn on the last bead in this circle, tie off the thread and firmly knot on the reverse side of the felt. (By this time you should have eight concentric circles of alternating colors of beads around the central blue bead.)

Step 11. Remove beaded felt from the hoop. With a pair of sharp scissors, *carefully* cut off the excess felt as close to the last circle of beads as you can. Ensure that you don't cut any of the threads that secure the last ring of beads.

Step 12. Glue psychic mandala onto the rock with household glue. Be sure of your placement. (If you can't find a suitable rock, glue the project to a flat piece of driftwood or some other natural object.) It is now ready for use.

Step 13. Hold the completed psychic mandala between your palms. Breathe deeply and close your eyes. Send it peaceful, soothing psychic energy.

When you wish to use the psychic mandala, light a blue candle. Place it behind and to one side of you so that its light shines onto the psychic mandala. Turn off all other lights in the room.

Gaze at the concentric circles. Say in a hushed voice:

Sacred circle of second sight,
with magic rings of nine;
bring me psychic visions tonight
while gazing at this sign.

Sit comfortably and contemplate the psychic mandala. Don't stare; gaze. Blink naturally if you wish. Soon your higher consciousness will be awakened. Be still and listen.

Night is the best time to promote psychic visions. Be sure that you're alone when you make the attempt.

CHAPTER SEVEN

A Pentacle, Protective Plaque, Runic Dice

CLAY, WHICH IS found throughout the world, was the first truly malleable substance used for art work and in the creation of utilitarian objects. This dense material, intimately connected with the earth, was transformed into a wide array of objects: images of goddesses and gods of all kinds; turtles and bison; winged griffins; pots, jars, and dishes in every size and shape imaginable, from petite drinking bowls to huge six-foot-tall storage containers. Pottery is much beloved by archaeologists, for the style of pottery found at digs at ancient sites is an accurate means of securing dates for prehistoric periods.

Though stone, ivory, and other more durable substances have long been worked as well, no substance but clay offered these early artists a truly flexible medium with which to create both ritual and mundane objects.

Clay's special properties, and the incredible transformations that it underwent in the hands of artisans, lent it extraordinary importance. Those who lived in earth-reverencing cultures saw clay as a divine substance. What material could be more perfectly suited to create deity images?

The craft of pottery probably began as early as the Neolithic period, the stratum at which the first pots are found, and this craft continues today. Ceramics from North America, England, Italy, Mexico, Spain, Fiji, China, and elsewhere continue to be prized objects, even when other, more permanent substances are available.

Clay was also the first paper. Throughout Mesopotamia, important business transactions, temple records, religious rites, and magical spells were recorded on clay. Many of these clay tablets, inscribed with cuneiform, have survived to this day.

In North America, clay was sacred. The Zuni thought of it as the body of a goddess. Because it possessed female energy all works involving clay, including pottery and brick making, were performed by women. Some of the finest living American Indian pottery artists are women.

Clay vessels are still used in religious and magical rites throughout the world. Why is this, when objects of metal, wood, glass, plastic, and stone are now available to us? Perhaps because clay is a gift from the earth, and the earth has been deemed to be sacred and holy.

Clay is much more than a sticky substance used in conventional craft work and art. It's a dense concentration of earth energies that we can use to create objects of magic.

Tools

The spell crafts in this chapter utilize few tools. Clay is available in a wide range of types and colors. It may be naturally found in your area. If not, purchase clay. It's best to use genuine clay for the purposes listed here. It can be air-dried until fairly hard but brittle. Careful handling will ensure that it doesn't break. If a clay object breaks, crumble it, return it to the earth, and create a new one— just as our ancestors did around the globe for untold generations.

Artificial "clays," such as the oily, oven-drying modeling types, aren't recommended. They're synthetic substances that lack magical qualities. Nonhardening modeling clays (such as Playdoh) also aren't recommended.

A toothpick, a whittled stick, or an awl can be used for drawing designs onto the clay. Since you're working with real clay you'll also need a small bowl of water to wet the clay and your fingers, and a towel for clean-up. You'll wish to work with clay on a flat, smooth surface, such as a tabletop covered with wax paper.

Check local craft and toy shops for sources of clay.

Procedures

Genuine clay is easiest to work with when moist, not wet. Try working with the clay with dry hands first. If it's too stiff, moisten your fingers and continue working.

To flatten clay, use the balls of the hands, pressing evenly. This speeds the process.

After making any object in this chapter, you'll be instructed to inscribe a design or runes onto it. Before doing this, let the newly made clay object "rest" for a few minutes, especially if you've wetted the clay. Have a damp paper towel nearby while inscribing, as you'll need to wipe off your inscribing tool after virtually every stroke.

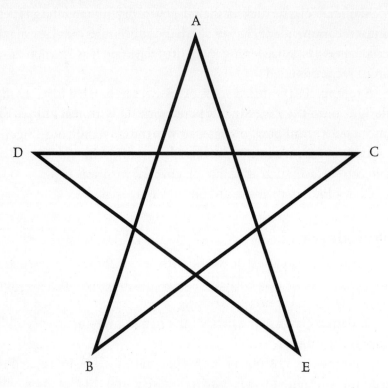

Money pentacle

Money Pentacle

Pentagrams have been used in magic throughout history. The pentagram's shape may have derived from the hand. This could account for its continued magical use for protection (hands are used to guard ourselves), as well as money (we earn our living with our hands).

The pentagram is an interlaced five-pointed star. Aside from its hand symbolism, it also represents the human body: the top point the head, the left and right middle points the arms, the bottom two the legs. Pentagrams were found among the ruins of Pompeii. It was in use even earlier, for a pot found at Tell Asmar (Jemdet Nasr period, circa 2750 B.C.E.) in Mesopotamia bears a painted pentagram. This figure is so steeped in magic, symbolism, and religion that of necessity these few words will have to suffice. (The pentagram isn't in any way connected with the Christian summation of evil.)

A pentacle (the term stems from ceremonial magic) is any round object decorated with a pentagram. This project utilizes the money-attracting properties of the pentagram.

Items needed:

> Clay
> Tracing paper
> Pencil or pen
> Inscribing tool (see introduction to chapter)

Break or cut off a tennis ball–sized piece of clay. Knead and roll it between the hands to form a ball. While doing this, visualize money coming into your life. On a piece of waxed paper, flatten the ball into a quarter-inch thick circle. Smooth the surface.

Transfer the diagram shown here to a piece of tracing paper. Lay it over the flat clay. If your clay disk is too large, roll it into a ball and flatten it again, adjusting it so that it is the correct width.

Using the toothpick or awl, poke a hole into the clay at each of the five outer points of the "star." Use these as guides when inscribing the pentagram onto the clay.

Remove the tracing paper. With your inscribing tool, draw a line across the surface of the clay from point A to point B, saying:

Money will come to me.

Saying these words each time, repeat from point B to point C, from point C to point D, from point D to point E, and finally from point E back to point A. You've just drawn a pentagram.

If the pentagram doesn't seem balanced, smooth over the surface of the clay, use the tracing paper to give you the starting points and try again.

When you're satisfied with the pentagram, let the pentacle dry on the waxed paper undisturbed for three days.

After the pentacle has dried, set it on a window sill, near the front door, or some other place in the home where it can remain undisturbed for a long period of time.

As you place the pentacle, say these or similar words while visualizing (which should be repeated at regular intervals):

> *Pentalpha, pentangel,*
> *It's money I need:*
> *Pentacle, pentagram,*
> *This is the seed!*

Home protection plaque

Home Protection Plaque

Items needed:

> Clay
> Pencil
> Inscribing instrument
> Sharp knife
> Red candle and holder

Visualize your home as a safe, protected environment as you charge the red candle. Light the candle, place it in its holder and set it near your work space.

Break off a piece of clay about the size of a golf ball. Knead the clay while visualizing your home as a protected refuge. Form the clay into a ball. Roll it between your hands until the clay forms a fat barrel shape, then place onto your working surface and smooth into a rough square.

Smooth with the fingers until the clay is of an even thickness (approximately one-quarter inch).

Using the pencil, make a hole clean through the clay approximately ½ inch from the edge of the clay. This will be used to hang the protective plaque.

Using the inscribing instrument, draw the runes and symbols on the example (page 53) onto the clay. Begin in the center of the square, leaving plenty of room for the rest of the runes.

Draw with power, visualizing your home as a fortress. If you draw incorrectly, simply smooth out the offending symbol or ball up the clay and begin again.

It will be necessary to clean your inscribing tool quite often. Work slowly. Turn the project so that you don't try to draw these runes upside-down.

The runes in the center of the plaque read: "Guard This House." The other four symbols are the astrological symbol for Saturn, the planet that rules the home.

When you've completed transferring the design to the center of your clay, trim off the right, bottom, and left edges of the clay, leaving a neat square shape (the top edge shouldn't be trimmed, as it has to be strong enough to support the plaque through its hole by hanging).

Let dry undisturbed for three days. Allow the red candle to burn out. When dry, pass a string or a piece of red yarn through the hole and hang the protective plaque inside your home near the front door while saying these or similar words:

My home is now
a fortress strong;
as day is light,
as night is long;
as long as night
comes after day,
my home is safe
in every way.

For Employment

Items needed:

> Clay
> Inscribing instrument

Form a small amount of clay into a ball. Flatten into a thin disk approximately one-eighth inch in thickness. As you work the clay, visualize yourself working a fulfilling, well-paying job.

Inscribe the design on the example above onto the clay:

Say these words as you inscribe:

> I *deserve to be happily, gainfully employed.*

Let the charm dry. When it has dried, take it outside. Break the thin employment disk and bury the pieces in the earth (or in a soil-filled flower pot) to release the power.

Repeat as needed for at least one week. It is done.

Employment charm

Divination Dice

Items needed:

> Clay
> Inscribing tool
> Blue candle

While visualizing your ability to accurately tune into your psychic abilities, form the clay into three small balls of equal size, approximately one inch in diameter. Flatten one ball so that it forms a cube (you may wish to push the side to be flattened against the waxed paper surface).

When all six sides have been flattened, lightly smooth the corners so that no very sharp edges remain.

Repeat the same procedure with the remaining two balls. All three dice should be of the exact same size, and should be as close to geometrically true cubes as you can manage.

With the inscribing instrument, draw the first four symbols shown on the following page onto one die, leaving the top and bottom of the die blank. Inscribe the next four onto the second die, and the last four onto the third die.

Let the dice dry until hard. To use them, charge a blue candle with psychic awareness and light its wick. Hold the dice in your power hand, thinking of your question or blanking your mind.

Roll the dice gently between your hands. Gently toss them onto a cloth-covered surface. (When dry, these dice are remarkably sturdy; we've dropped them on the floor without causing them any damage.) The symbols visible on the top of each die determine your possible future.

Divination dice

One, two, or three symbols may appear. Read them together. For example, the "Wealth" symbol next to the "Disordered Thoughts" symbol could indicate that you're worrying too much about money, or that your mind is blocking the arrival of money into your life. "Conflict" appearing with "End" may mean that an expected confrontation won't occur. If only one symbol appears, it's of vital importance. Allow the symbol to tell your psychic mind what you need to know. If no symbols appear, try again.

Keep in mind your question while studying the dice. With practice, this can be an easy method of divination.

When you're finished with the reading, quench the blue candle's flame. Relight it each time you consult the dice. When it's burned out, charge another for this purpose.

(Note: if, after drying, one of the die virtually always turns up the same symbol, it's unevenly balanced. Another should be made.)

These are the twelve symbols, but feel free to create your own set of symbols:

The Home

Family relations, foundation, and stability, your immediate environment, your inner self.

Possessions

Tangible objects, the material world, unhealthy relationships, the mundane.

Love

Relationships, romance, mates, self-image, friendships.

Poison

Gossip, negative thoughts, baneful habits, harmful attitudes, slander, guilt, jealousy, envy.

Wealth

Money, financial concerns, savings, employment, employers, loans, credit, security.

Disordered Thoughts

Emotional tension, irrationality, confusion, doubt, insecurity.

Woman

A female, women, the inner-female self, women's mysteries.

Man

A man, men, the inner-male self, men's mysteries.

Gift

Legacies, promotions, windfalls, physical talents, physical abilities, psychic and spiritual gifts, sacrifices, volunteering, giving of oneself.

Comfort

Ease, pleasure, happiness, peace, joy, a turn for the better.

End

The end of a matter, a new beginning, change, initiation, purification.

Conflict

Arguments, struggles, hostility, aggression, anger, confrontations.

CHAPTER EIGHT

Ojos and a Shaman's Arrow

THE MIRACLE OF sight is often thought to be the most precious of the five senses. Early humans regarded eyes as wondrous objects filled with magic, and reverence for eyesight has been expressed since the earliest ages.

An ancient religious site excavated in Mesopotamia became known as the "eye temple" due to the thousands of votive figures found within it. These figures, which were made in about 3000 B.C.E., are dominated by large, mystical eyes. The votive images probably represent worshipers; their wide stares demonstrate their eagerness to view and to be seen by the gods. Even at the dawn of civilization, early peoples had firmly linked the eyes with one of our species' most basic needs: worship of the divine.

Early human existence was a constant struggle against overwhelming odds. Floods, drought-produced famine, and mysterious illnesses were some of the natural forces that seemed to be working against early humans. Such destructive forces were personified as evil spirits and demons.

Eventually, another belief came into existence: that persons or spirits could inflict harm simply with a glance. This curious belief, which associated the eyes with negative energy, became known as the "evil eye."

To keep both evil spirits and the evil eye at bay, humans began constructing and wearing certain amulets. Most of such amulets always bore a resemblance to the eye. Some were anatomically correct, such as the eyes painted on the prows of ships to guard them from harm. Others, created by winding thread or yarn around crossed sticks, were more abstract, but still retained the protective and spiritual power of the eyes. These latter constructions are today known as thread crosses, or *ojos de dios* (Spanish for "god's eyes").

Though best known as Pagan religious tools made by the Huichols in the Narayit state of Mexico, similar objects were also made in such distant places as Africa, France, Sweden, Denmark, Germany, Australia, Tibet, and China. The Huichols make god's eyes to this day to draw the attention of the gods to successful ventures, for general blessing purposes, and as votive offerings to their deities. They're made so that the eyes of the deities will rest on the worshipers. Elsewhere in the world, these thread crosses were used to trap ghosts or spirits, to drive out illness, and to confer protection.

The words "god" and "cross" should be addressed here. Such tools were made centuries before the spread of Christianity, and have no connections with the Christian concept of "God." Similarly, though the cross is the most common symbol of Christianity, its use in religion is far older; originally, crosses were solar or phallic symbols. Thus, "god's eyes" or "thread crosses" have no connection with Christianity—they're a purely Pagan tool.

Some have seen in these devices a symbolic watching by the deity (or deities). Others simply see them as magical protectants with no direct spiritual connections. The choice is yours, for both views are correct.

In this chapter we'll be making both a thread cross and an object that includes a thread cross as part of its design. Such magical tools make excellent gifts for friends as well as potent protectants.

Health and Well-Being God's Eye

Items needed:

> 1 skein blue yarn
> 1 skein purple yarn
> 2 10-inch sticks (small dowels, wooden skewers,
>   or Popsicle sticks)
> Scissors

Step 1. To begin, place one stick over the center of the other to form an equal-armed cross.

Step 2. Wrap the blue yarn under C end of stick, over the cross of the sticks, and again over the cross.

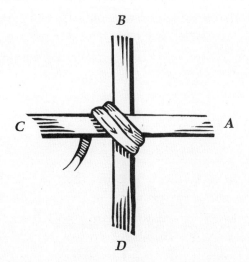

Step 3. Pass the yarn behind the B end of stick and then wrap it over the cross in the opposite direction twice. This holds the sticks together and will start your eye.

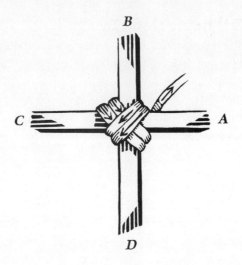

Step 4. Now that the center has been finished, begin creating the "eye." Pass the yarn in front of the D end of stick and wrap it over and around the end of stick A. Rotate a quarter turn clockwise.

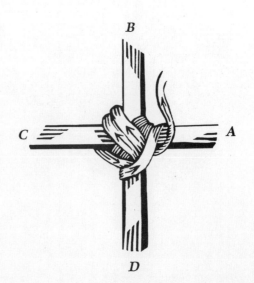

Step 5. Repeat wrapping and rotating quarter turn until you've covered half the length of the sticks. As you do this, visualize protection. If you find this difficult, concentrate on the winding of the yarn.

Step 6. When you've covered half of the sticks, tie the end of the blue yarn to the stick. Trim excess with the scissors. Tie the purple yarn to the stick and continue building up your eye.

Step 7. Repeat this pattern until the eye is completed.

Hang your new ojo in your home. As you do so, say these or similar words:

> *I now place this threaded sign*
> *for health in spirit and in mind.*

Completed ojo

Shaman's Arrow

Shaman's arrows are used as messengers to the ancient gods. Made by the Huichols of Mexico, such arrows are never actually shot (at the gods or toward any living person). Instead, they're hung up (or inserted into the thatch) in the home, placed on altars, worn, or are thrust into the ground.

These arrows are actually prayer messengers. Once made, they continuously convey the most fervent prayers of their crafters. Such arrows are made in great quantities and are found wherever the Huichols worship: in the mountains, in caves, near springs, rivers, lakes, and the ocean.

For special blessings, miniature objects are often tied onto the arrows: a woman may attach a tiny pair of sandals to express her desire for a husband, or a hunter may hang a small representation of a deer from the arrow for a successful hunt.

The most beautiful of the objects attached to the prayer arrows are the feathers and plumes of a variety of birds. These feathers increase the arrows' power and their speed in "flying" to the gods. They also represent specific Huichol deities.

Huichol prayer arrows consist of a bamboo shaft into which a long piece of hardwood is inserted. Besides the decorations mentioned above, the rear shaft is usually decorated with painted bands that represent specific deities.

Our version of a shaman's arrow described below is made to enhance spirituality of any kind. It can be used to send prayers to the deities. Though we suggest hanging it in your home, it can also be pushed into the ground outside in wild places. Wherever it is placed, it should be placed with reverence.

Shaman's arrow

Items needed:

    1 skein red yarn
    1 skein black yarn
    2 10-inch long sticks (or thin dowels)
    1 25-inch natural twig or tree branch (find one that has nat-
        urally fallen from a tree and leave an offering in its place)
    Feathers (fallen feathers gathered on walks, feathers dropped
        by pet birds—parrot feathers are quite beautiful)
    Scissors

Step 1. Using the instructions for the "Health and Well-Being Ojo," make an eye with the two ten-inch sticks. Begin by using black yarn. The black center of the eye should extend for one-half inch. Then wrap red yarn for about one inch. End with about one inch of black yarn. (If you can't visualize spiritually while working with the yarn, at least keep the reason for creating the arrow in mind.)

Step 2. Tie the red yarn to the wider end of the branch with a knot. Wrap the red yarn carefully around the branch toward you, ensuring that the branch is being covered. Do this for 1 inch, then tie off the red yarn.

Step 3. Knot black yarn and wrap for one inch.

Step 4. Repeat, alternating colors, until ten inches of the branch have been covered with yarn. Secure the yarn with a knot.

Step 5. Attach the ojo to the branch. To attach, tie a piece of black yarn to one of the ojo sticks, and tie the other end of the yarn to the middle of the yarn-wrapped portion of the stick. There should be about one inch of yarn between the hanging and the stick.

Step 6. To complete the shaman's arrow, push the bare ends of the feathers under the yarn at the starting point of the yarnwrap on the branch. Glue isn't necessary to hold them in place.

Step 7. To use your shaman's arrow to enhance spirituality, hang it in the home in a prominent place with these or similar words:

Beings of the sky, wind, and ground,
bless this arrow I've tightly wound.
Spirituality come forth:
come from the east, south, west, and north!

CHAPTER NINE

Sand Painting

MANY HAVE HEARD of the sand paintings created by Navajo shamans. These are intricate representations of deities and sacred symbols, created by carefully pouring sands of various colors onto the ground. Sand paintings are usually created for use in healing ceremonies, and are destroyed after the ritual. They're an impermanent, yet beautiful form of spiritually inspired art.

Though sand paintings are made in other parts of the world (in Tibet, for example), those created by the Navajo are the best known. Made with crushed and ground sandstone of various colors, they're an important part of the Navajo heritage.

Those of us who aren't Navajo, and aren't Navajo shamans, can't (and shouldn't) create Navajo sand paintings. We can, however, use the technique to create similarly unique, temporary art works for specific ritual purposes.

The sand painting that we'll discuss in this chapter is a type of image magic. This age-old technique is quite simple: the magician creates a physical representation of the needed spell's goal. This object is then used in dramatic ritual during which personal power is sent forth to effect the change.

In sand painting, we use the medium of colored sand to create images of our goals. Because these figures are delicate and temporary, a new sand painting is created for each use.

You may wish to practice "drawing" with sand before trying the rituals contained within this chapter. This form of spell craft requires a steady hand. *One last note*: the larger your sand paintings are, the easier it will be to follow these instructions.

Materials needed for sand painting

The Materials

Sand paintings, naturally, require colored sand or some other finely grained substance that is available in several colors. In the United States, green, black, red, coral-yellow, gray, brown, and white sands can be found. Beaches, deserts, dry river beds, and volcanic areas are treasure troves of such substances. Sandstone of various colors can also be ground to sand.

Semiprecious stones may also be crushed to create "sands." Recently we accidentally made purple sand by washing a specimen of the lithium-rich mineral, lepidolite. It promptly crumbled to a sparkling, purple sand.

If colored sands are out of your reach, you can easily make your own. To do this, you needn't gather white sand and dye it. Simply use normal table salt. That's right, that crystal that we use in our food.

The process is easy. Obtain a set of four food colorings: red, green, yellow, and blue. (The squeeze bottles are fine. If you wish to use the larger glass containers of food coloring, buy an eye-dropper as well.)

Place one cup plain table salt in a small bowl. Add seven or so drops of food coloring to the salt. Stir with a spoon until the salt is evenly tinted.

Repeat with the remaining three colors in three separate bowls of salt. You'll have four different colored "sands" to be used in the following rituals.

A fourth color is required for this chapter: purple. Purple is easily made by mixing equal parts of red and blue. Mix the food colorings in a spoon and then add to the salt. (Don't add the colors separately.)

Where white sand is called for, leave it uncolored. Naturally, if you do have red, yellow, blue, green, and purple sand, fine. Use them. If not, feel free to utilize the colored salts. They're just as effective as sands for our purposes.

Sand Painting for a Peaceful House

Sands needed:

> White
> Blue
> Purple

This sand painting is created when the house is disturbed from inside or outside influences. Its purpose is to resolve the conflicts that are creating the disturbances.

Create the sand painting, if possible, on a bare floor within the house itself. A living room, a bedroom, even the kitchen will do. (Sand paintings can't be made on carpeted surfaces.) If you have no uncarpeted sections of floor that can be used, make this sand painting on a large table.

The night before the ritual, sweep (and, if necessary, mop) the area in which you'll make the sand painting. Dye the salts as well, if you haven't any on hand. (Dyed salts may cake overnight if left exposed to the air. Simply break up the clumps with a spoon.)

The next morning, preferably at dawn, rise and quietly bathe. Dry yourself, dress in clean clothing, and take the salts to the ritual area.

Kneel or sit on the floor. Close your eyes and visualize your home as a stronghold of peace, calm, and love. After a few moments open your eyes and begin.

Pick up the white sand. Pour a small quantity of it into the palm of your power hand. Move your hand to within an inch or two of the floor and tilt it so that a small stream of sand falls from it. With this sand create an outline of your home. You're not making a blueprint; simply a recognizable shape. If you live in an apartment or attached condominium, draw the front view of your own unit as opposed to the entire building.

As you do this say these or similar words:

Here is my home.

Add more sand to your palm as necessary and keep pouring the sand until the outline has been completed.

Next, brush off your palm and pour blue sand onto it. Create an endless circle around your home. Starting above its roof, move clockwise around the image. The circle doesn't have to touch the image of your house.

As you do this say these or similar words:

Here is my home in peace.

Brush off your hand and fill it with purple sand. Make another, larger circle around the blue sand circle, this time touching it. Make the circle as perfect as you can. As you do this say these or similar words:

Here is my home in serenity.

When you've finished the purple circle, gaze down at the painting that you have created. Your home is surrounded with peace and serenity As you look at the picture, fix that image in your mind. Build personal power. Send it into the picture, into the image, and the rings of peace. See them vibrating and glowing with soothing, peaceful energies.

Using a small broom, sweep up the sands and place them into a small white cloth. Tie up the ends and place this peaceful charm somewhere in your home.

A Healing Sand Painting

Sands needed:

> Blue
> White
> Yellow
> Red
> Purple

Perform this ritual on a floor prepared as in the above rite. This is a self-healing. It simply can't be effective for any other person.

Place the sands before you. Visualize yourself in perfect emotional, spiritual, and physical health. See yourself vibrating with the radiance of health. Build personal power. Pour the blue sand into your power hand. Create a square with the blue sand on the floor at least two feet wide. Say these or similar words as you do this:

Here is latent healing energy.

Dust off your hand and pour white sand into your power hand. In the center of the blue square begin to pour the sand, clockwise, to create an outline of a human being (yourself). Visualize this outline as being you. As you do this, say these or similar words:

Here is my body—blocked, unhealed.

Dust off your hand. Take up the yellow sand. Pour a bit into the head portion of the figure. Say:

Here is my mind—perfectly functioning,
vital, free of negative thoughts.

Dust off your hand. Pick up the red sand. Pour some of it into the chest area of the figure. Say:

Here is my heart—perfectly functioning,
filled with love, free of guilt, forgiving of myself.

Dust off your hand. Pick up the purple sand. Create an "aura" with it around the human figure, an outline in purple touching the white. Do this in a clockwise direction. Say these or similar words:

Here is my spirit—attuned with flesh and mind.

Dust off your hand. With your projective hand, "bend" inward the corners of the outer blue square. Work slowly as you do this—

upper right, lower right, lower left, upper left. Transform the square of latent healing energy into a circle of active healing energy.

Gaze down at the completed figure. You glow with health. You are complete. Healed. Visualize.

Say these or similar words:

> Here is my body—unblocked, healed.
> My thoughts are free and positive.
> My love is strong and free of guilt.
> My spirit is attuned.
> Healing energy bursts into manifestation.

See the graphic demonstration of your changed condition. Feel its energy radiating up into you from the sand painting.

Move away the bowls of salt, if they're nearby. Lie on the sand painting facedown, pressing your stomach into the painting. Accept its loving, healing energies into your body. Feel the effects they have on your inner self, releasing the blockages (of mind or emotions) that have created the illness or other condition.

Slide up and down on the painting, dispersing the design and releasing its power into you.

When finished, dust yourself off, sweep up the sand and place in a large container. Repeat this entire ritual once a day for at least a week.

As to the colored salts left over after the rituals: add three teaspoons to each bath until the supply has been exhausted.

A Prosperity Sand Painting

Items needed:*

> Green sand
> Green candle and holder
> Five pennies
> Freshly dug earth

* The candle, holder, pennies, and earth aren't necessary until seven days after you've performed this ritual.

This sand painting should be created on a flat surface on which it can remain for at least a week. (A large, flat dish might be appropriate. Use your imagination.)

Sit or stand before the area with the sand. Visualize. Build personal power. Pour the green sand into your projective hand.

Working carefully and slowly, forming a pentagram (see chapter 7) with the sand. Beginning at the top point, move down to the lower left point, up to the upper right, across to the upper left, down to the lower right, and back up to the top point to complete the pentagram.

Visualize throughout this procedure. When finished, say:

> *Prosperity, prosperity,*
> *prosperity shall come to me.*

Once you've finished making the pentagram, pour the green sand in a circle surrounding and touching the pentagram, working clockwise as usual.

Then, while still visualizing increased money in your life, pour a square of green sand—in a clockwise motion—around the circle.

You've created a pentagram within a circle within a square.

See the money energy lying there. It breathes and writhes within the green sand, waiting to be released. To do this, charge a large green candle with money energies. Place in a holder and set in the center of the pentagram. Light the wick and chant the following or similar words:

> *Money lies within this sign,*
> *money's here now; money's mine.*

As you chant, see the pentagram's energy streaming out in three-dimensional form, rocketing to the sky and then raining down on you.

Afterward, pinch or snuff out the flame and leave the candle and sand painting in place. Every day for the following six days, relight the candle, chant the words, and visualize for a few minutes.

After the final chant on the seventh day, scatter the sand painting with your projective hand to release any last vestiges of energy. Sweep up the green sand, add five pennies and a handful of freshly dug earth, mix together, and keep in a bar or box in your home.

Repeat as necessary.

Completed prosperity sand painting

CHAPTER TEN

The Corn Mother

GRAIN HAS ALWAYS been reverenced. The importance of these plants that provide such a basic food have firmly established them in the realms of magic, religion, and spirituality. In Asia, rice was honored. Throughout Europe, wheat was the sustaining grain (see chapter 21). Oats were blessed and honored in Scotland. Millet has been cultivated with prayer and ritual in Africa for 6,000 years. In the Americas, corn played an unquestionably important role in the physical and spiritual lives of the inhabitants.

Across the continent and as far south as Latin America, corn was divine. In the Yucatan region of Mexico, corn is still sacred. It's planted with prayers to the *yuntzilob* (the pre-Christian deities) and is under their protection. While growing, corn isn't mentioned by its name *ixim* but is termed *aracia*, the word used to describe the spiritual essence of offerings made to the deities.

Thrashing around in a corn field, throwing corn on the ground, or cracking dried kernels between the teeth; such actions are thought to be extremely disrespectful in the Yucatan. Corn is truly the staff of life among these peoples; as such, it's respected and linked with divinity.

Similar views were common among most Plains Indian tribes of North America. Indeed, Corn Mother enjoyed worship as a deity among many peoples.

The Pueblo held that the corn represented the earth, the sky, and the body. The ear is seen to be female; the sweet, whitish juice pressed from fresh kernels is the milk that nourishes humans and animals. The tassels of the flowering plant are viewed as male. The spiral pattern seen in the kernels of an ear of corn certainly contributed to this grain's aura of sanctity.

The Zuni viewed corn as a sacred substance, and related corn of various colors to the four directions. The sacred stories of various American Indian tribes are rife with legends and tales concerning the Corn Mother. Whole religions were centered around this worship.

To the peoples that honored her, the Corn Mother wasn't simply a mythic figure. She was the Goddess of Plenty providing sustaining food. She was real, and her worshipers knew this every time they ate corn.

Making the Corn Mother

The Corn Mother that we'll be creating is Southwestern American Indian in origin. We found it in an old book dating from the late 1800s concerning American Indian traditions. This Corn Mother was made for the purpose of bringing peace and happiness to the home.

Items needed:

> 1 ear dried Indian corn with colorful kernels (available in markets during the fall, or check florist or craft shops)
> 1 round, wooden base approximately 5" x 5" in diameter (check craft stores)

Items needed to make a Corn Mother

½-inch, wide-headed nail
1 skein natural, off-white wool (not synthetic) yarn*
12 feathers†
Household glue (optional)
Hammer
Corn meal
A small bowl

---

* Home-spun wool yarn is best, but many types can be bought in stores. The texture of home-spun yarns makes this project more pleasingly rustic. Earthy colors are best.

† Use small, fallen feathers. Collecting them while on a walk through the countryside is an exciting and healthful practice. If you share your life with birds, their fallen feathers may also be collected and used for the decoration. Feathers can be bought in stores, but avoid using those that have been dyed. See part 3 for more feather information.

Step 1. Begin by placing the base on two bricks, books, or rocks (see illustration), bottom side up. Hammer the nail through the center of the base until the nail head is flush with the bottom of the base.

Step 2. Turn over the base. Spread glue about one-half inch wide around the nail. (Optional. This anchors the project into place.)

Step 3. Unhusk dried Indian corn, if necessary. Holding the corn, very carefully push the stem end of the ear onto the nail. *Carefully* force the corn entirely onto the nail, so that the stem end of the ear rests on the top of the base, and the thin end points straight up.

Step 4. Apply a light coating of household glue to your hands and apply to the cob (to ensure that the yarn will adhere to it). (Optional. This makes it much easier for the yarn to adhere to the ear.)

Step 5. Tie one end of the yarn around the base of the corn cob with a tight knot. Push knot under cob, if possible. Now, wind the yarn around the ear from the base to the top. Repeat this several times until the colored corn kernels are completely covered.

Step 6. Place the feathers into the top of the yarn-wrapped ear in a pleasing pattern that resembles a headdress. Work with this for a while until you've found the best pattern. You might wish to put five or seven feathers standing straight up (to resemble a headdress) and some on either side to hang down like hair or earrings. Real wool yarn will hold the feathers in place without glue.

Step 7. Dedicate the Corn Mother. Hold her up to the north, charge her with peaceful energies, and say these or similar words:

Powers of the north!
Bless this Corn Mother!

Hold her up to the east, charge her with peace and happiness, and say these or similar words:

Powers of the east!
Bless this Corn Mother!

Hold her up to the south, charge her with peace and happiness, and say:

Powers of the south!
Bless this Corn Mother!

Corn Mother

Hold her up to the west, charge her with peace and happiness, and say:

Powers of the west!
Bless this Corn Mother!

Place the Corn Mother in her new home. This should be a spot of some prominence, such as the kitchen table, the mantel, or some other place.

Fill a bowl with corn meal. Slowly sprinkle a circle of corn meal three times around the Corn Mother while saying:

May this Corn Mother bless our home
with happiness and peace.

It is done.

CHAPTER ELEVEN

Tapers of Power

LIGHT IS AN ancient magical tool. Associated with the sun, seen on stormy nights dancing in the clouds as well as in the stars and moon overhead, light has been an aspect of religious and magical rituals for uncounted years.

Fire was the earliest form of light that humans could produce at will. Crackling bonfires cooked food, provided warmth, and frightened off dangerous animals, but they were also the centerpiece for mystic rites. The very creation of fire (using wood or stone and combustible plant materials) was suffused with magic.

Fire making was one of the earliest magical secrets. Cultures throughout history have told stories of how humans (or animals) stole fire from above, or discovered the secret of its making from divine or semidivine beings. Eventually, knowledge of this process became widespread.

But fire didn't lose its magic. Burning sticks and torches were used in rites of all types. Later, oil lamps graced altars throughout the Old

World. Ancient Hebrew magicians directed preadolescent boys to gaze into flames to divine the future. Lamps were lit to invoke the blessings of deities or to work for magical purposes. Bonfires were ignited on hilltops and in secret places both to light and to lend power to spells.

Fire was sacred because it contained light. Light was sacred because it created and sustained life. Fire, then, was a perfect symbol of divinity and of power.

Candles of beeswax or tallow were in vogue during classical Rome (we've found no trace of their use in either ancient Greece or Egypt), but oil lamps were thought to be purer and more suitable for magical and spiritual use. Eventually, though, beeswax candles came to be accepted in many religions, and tens of thousands of candles burn today on religious altars. Only candles of pure beeswax or petroleum are used for this purpose. Candles of tallow (which are unavailable in the United States) are still considered to be "unclean."

Within the last 100 years, candles have become an accepted and important aspect of folk magic. Candles are currently made in a bewildering variety of shapes, sizes, and colors, each suited to a specific magical purpose.

Mass-produced candles can certainly be used for magical rites, but the joys of candle making, the pride in using tapers that you've created with magical intent, and the extra energies that they contain, make this a particularly satisfying spell craft.

Candles are simple to make, require few special tools or materials, and are powerful focal points for visualization and personal power.

You can certainly run to the store to purchase candles for rituals, but those you've made yourself will personalize your magic to an even greater extent.

The Wax

Beeswax is the best material. It has the longest history and, as the product of bees, is intimately linked with nature. Unfortunately, it's also expensive and rather difficult to find in quantity unless you tend beehives.

The only alternative is paraffin, which is produced from petroleum. Petroleum, as we all know, is growing rather scarce. Within a decade or so beeswax may be less expensive than paraffin. Either can be used. (Because paraffin is widely available, these instructions have been written using paraffin.)

The early American colonists made bayberry candles. True bayberry candles are rare today. Bayberry wax is collected by boiling the berries of this American shrub. A waxy substance rises on the water. This is skimmed off and made into candles. Enormous quantities of bayberries are required to make a single candle, but the evocative fragrance of bayberries made these tapers quite popular. Though once an important source of light, bayberry candles are today burned to attract money.

For suppliers of beeswax and other candle-making equipment, check your local craft stores, markets (for paraffin), and the appendix of this book.

Money Candles

Items needed:

> 2–4 pounds paraffin (the kind that markets sell for use in canning)
> Thin candlewicking
> Green candle dye (or a green crayon)
> ½ teaspoon ground cinnamon
> ½ teaspoon ground nutmeg
> A small bowl

Patchouly essential oil

A large pot and a smaller can (a coffee can works well; the
taller the can, the longer your tapers will be; a tall, thin
can, slightly longer than the length you desire your candles to be, is ideal)

Baking soda (for fire safety)

1 wooden spoon

Waxed paper

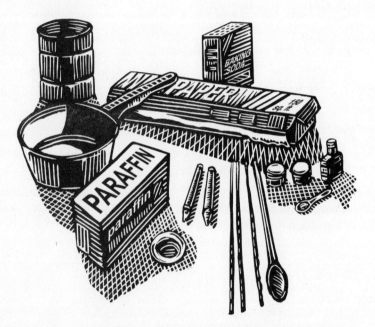

Ingredients for making candles

Step 1. To speed the melting process, grate or chop the wax into small pieces before melting. Fill the large pot about one-third full of water. Place on high heat until boiling. Place the paraffin in the can, and set the can into the pot.

Turn the heat down to medium. Watch the wax as it's melting. Paraffin easily bursts into flame over high heat (this is exactly why it's used to make candles). If flames appear, place a lid over the can or drench the area with baking soda to snuff out the fire. If you keep the heat low, you should have no problems.

Step 2. While the wax is melting, place the two spices into the bowl. Mix them together, empowering them as you visualize money manifesting in your life. Infuse the herbs with your goal.

Step 3. Check the wax. For best results, you should have at least six inches of melted wax. If there's less, add more wax. (If the wax has melted, but has begun to harden, the heat is too low. Turn it up a bit.)

Add a few chunks of green candle dye to the wax and mix with the wooden spoon. Alternately, remove the paper wrappings from a green crayon, break it into pieces, and add this to the wax.

The dye will melt. Stir until the paraffin is evenly colored. The finished, dried candles will be a shade or two lighter than the color of the melted wax. More dye may be necessary to create the desired dark green shade.

Step 4. Once the wax has been tinted, sprinkle the spices onto the wax with your projective hand. Dust off your fingers over the pot and stir the herbs into the wax with the wooden spoon. Stir clockwise and visualize.

Add eight to sixteen drops patchouly essential oil to the wax and again stir with the wooden spoon.

Smell the wax. It should be heavily scented. If not, add more patchouly oil.

Step 5. Begin dipping. Hold a length of cotton wicking between your thumb and forefinger. Dunk it into the wax. It'll probably just float on the surface the first few times you do this, for the wick lacks enough weight to plunge it to the bottom of the pan. After dipping, remove it and hold it in the air for a moment or two until the wax has set, then dip again.

Dip again, lift the wicking completely from the melted wax, allow the wax to set, and redip. Repeat as needed. The longer you wait between drippings, allowing the wax to harden, the faster the candle will build up. If you simply dunk and dunk and dunk, the hot paraffin will melt each proceeding coat and you'll end up with a soggy piece of wick.

With proper dipping, the candle will soon form. Its bottom will grow into an inverted-cone shape from the wax that drips down the taper's sides as it cools. This is natural; don't worry about it.

Step 6. When the candle has achieved the proper width, hang it to dry in a spot where it won't be touched for several minutes. We usually stick the top of the wick under the bottom of a cupboard door and shut the door, thus allowing the candle to hang freely.

Test the candle after twenty or so minutes. The wax should have set but the taper should still be warm. Check it periodically to be sure that it hasn't completely hardened before the next step.

Step 7. Turn off the heat under the wax. Smooth out the waxed paper on a counter or table. Lay the candle on the paper and gently, with an easy rocking motion, roll the candle back and forth on the waxed paper. This straightens the taper and reduces irregularities on its surface.

Step 8. When the candle is fairly straight, cut off the inverted cone at the bottom of the candle with a sharp knife. Dip the

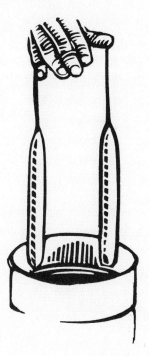

Dipping the candles

taper two more times into the melted wax and hang to dry until hard. You've just made a money spell candle. (To save time and produce more tapers, make two, three, or four at a time. Hang each to dry as you dip the next. This may require the construction of a drying rack or the use of many cupboards: one candle per cupboard avoids accidents—the horror of your freshly made candles plunging to the floor and smashing themselves.)

Step 9. To use your money spell candle, choose a time when you'll be alone. Smell the rich, prosperous scent and visualize money manifesting in your life.

Hold the candle tightly between your palms. Send energy into it, saying something like the following words:

I charge you by Jupiter,
I charge you by the earth,
I charge you by the sun, moon, and stars:
bring money to me,
prosperity.
Money to me,
prosperity.
Money to me,
prosperity.

Set the candle in a holder. Light it. Sit or stand before it, watching the flame transform the wax into a liquid. Visualize the candle releasing the energies that you've placed within it. Sense it sending out power to bring your need for money into manifestation.

Let the candle burn down to its end (if in a safe location). Or, allow it to burn for four, eight, or sixteen minutes daily until your need manifests.

Other Types of Spell Candles

The same ritual and processes can be used to create candles for any magical purpose. Recommended colors, herbs or spices, and oils suited to many of these goals follow, but feel free to experiment. Grind all herbs before using, and use only genuine essential oils (see the appendix for suppliers).

Health

Blue candle dye
Allspice
Sage
Sandalwood oil

Love

A bit of red candle dye (this will dye the wax pink)
Rose petals
Basil
Lavender oil

Protection

No dye; leave the wax white
Rosemary
Sage
Frankincense (or cedar) oil

Psychic Awareness

Blue candle dye
Lemongrass
Yarrow
Lemon oil

Purification

No dye; leave the wax white
Anise
Lemon peel
Lavender oil

Spirituality

Purple candle dye (if unavailable, leave white)
Myrrh
Cinnamon
True jasmine oil (which is quite expensive) or sandalwood oil

CHAPTER TWELVE

A Spell Broom

BROOMS ARE ANCIENT tools of magic. European folklore is filled with tales of brooms and their ritual uses. Though often associated with Witches, brooms can be found in virtually every household in every country in the world. Each day, millions of these bristled tools are used in quite ordinary ways. Why, then, do they possess such a mystic aura?

This is revealed by a look at the broom's function. Brooms are used to sweep. Sweeping cleans; it purifies. That, we believe, is the origin of the broom's magical power—its usefulness in purification.

Most of us grew up around flat Shaker-type brooms, the most common type in the United States today. Round brooms, while attractive, aren't as effective in performing their simple mission, and so flat brooms have all but overtaken their round counterparts. Though we've virtually lost the round broom, most of these sweeping devices (save for a few) are still made of natural materals: a wooden handle, broomcorn (for the sweeping end), a nail, and wire.

Round brooms are still made today, in limited quantities, by craftspeople in the United States. In other countries, round brooms are still in common use.

Magically, round brooms are emblematic of the moon and of its energies, as well as of women, water, and the earth itself. Then, too, round brooms are evocative of past times, when magic was an accepted part of life and when the broom was a tool of this ancient art. Therefore, we'll be discussing the creation of round brooms.

This chapter describes the creation of a temporary round broom. Such brooms are made for a specific magical purpose, then are disassembled and returned to the earth. Though spell brooms can be used for a variety of magical purposes, we'll be making a purification broom in this chapter. As with all magical crafts, the end purpose of the broom should be visualized throughout the creation process.

You'll be making short brooms. Longer brooms can certainly be created by adjusting the sizes of the stick and sweeps, but the smaller size seems to be the easiest to use.

All types of spell brooms are made in exactly the same way. The materials used determine the broom's specific energies. These brooms require fresh plant materials.

Purification Broom

A home purification may be necessary for a variety of reasons: strife within the household, the temporary absence of a mate, simple tension, or just plain bad vibes. Winter and spring are also traditional times to perform a household purification (some magicians also perform a household purification at each New Moon).

Items needed:

1 fallen tree branch, approximately ¼ inch in diameter, and 1 foot long (or 1 dowel, ¼ inch by 1 foot)
A bowl of water
Raffia
Scissors

Fresh bunches of one or more of any of the following plants: broom, cedar, fennel, lavender, peppermint, rosemary, pepper tree (*Schinus molle*). (This last plant grows throughout the Southwestern United States, and is a traditional ingredient in similar magical implements made in Mexico.)

Items needed to make a spell broom

Step 1. Collect the plant materials. You need only one of these plants, but can use more than one if you wish. Ideally, these will be from your own garden. If not, roam the countryside with a good field guide to plants (available from your local library). Or, check your local market—many are now stocking fresh herbs, and rosemary is usually available.

After finding the plant(s), cut a few branches from each, leaving plenty of growth so that the plant can survive. Collect with love. (Do this with the collection formula as outlined in chapter 3.)

Step 2. Find a fallen branch of about the correct size or, failing this, buy a dowel.

Step 3. Assemble your tools: the plants, the branch, the raffia; and the scissors. Charge the plant materials with purifying energy, visualizing them sweeping away negativity, sweeping in positive energies.

Step 4. Charge the broomstick (the branch or dowel) by placing it between your hands and sending purifying energies into it.

Step 5. Tie one end of a long piece of raffia around the bottom of the broomstick. As you tie the knot, say:

I *tie in purification.*

Step 6. Take four or five stalks of the plant material (it's difficult to say exactly how much to use; this depends on the plant selected.) Place the stem ends against the end of the broom stick, over the tied raffia, with the leafy ends extending downward, away from the stick. Wrap the raffia tightly around the broomstick and plant material. Visualize.

Step 7. Place another bunch of plant material beside the first and tightly wrap the raffia around it. Visualize purification. Repeat until you've completely covered the end of the broomstick with the plants, each time tightly wrapping the raffia around them directly over the last raffia layer.

If the sweeping end doesn't seem full enough, add more plant material using the same technique.

Step 8. When the broom has been made, push the loose end of the raffia under the last two or so layers of raffia (using a stick, a fork, or the scissors) and tie. Snip off the end of the raffia. If desired, trim the short ends of the plant materials with the scissors. The broom is now ready for use.

Step 9. Place your projective hand over the bowl of water and say these or similar words while visualizing:

Completed purification broom

Water of water,
wash it clean;
both that which is seen
and unseen.

Sprinkle water onto the sweeps of the broom. Walk to the front door of your home. Open it (if possible) and vigorously brush the air in front of it, driving away negativity. (You needn't actually sweep the floor; only the air above it.) Visualize as you brush. Close the door.

Moving clockwise through the house, sweep away at all windows, doors, and other entrances. Sweep in both the upper and lower corners of all rooms. This should take several minutes.

When you've finished, sweep at the front door again. Raise the broom, vigorously shake it three times, and lay it before the front door for nine minutes. After this, untie the raffia, take apart the broom and, at the soonest possible time, bury the plant materials, raffia, and stick outside.

It is done.

CHAPTER THIRTEEN

A Protective "Hex" Sign

THROUGHOUT SOUTHEASTERN PENNSYLVANIA, barns and other farm buildings often feature brightly painted, circular designs. Though these designs are found in great variation, they usually include symbols such as rosettes, hearts, tulips, raindrops, oak leaves, stars, and goldfinches. These symbols, known as "hex signs," have been created for well over 100 years.

They're of obscure origin. Some say that the intricate, beautifully detailed signs are mere decoration, perhaps inspired by quilt patterns. Others say that they were originally painted onto farm buildings to show that they were covered by fire insurance (this was before 1800), or as an emblem of land ownership. Some even state that they're religious symbols.

Still, one fact is clear: Pennsylvania Dutch hex signs are magical in nature, and still retain their energies. They've become so popular that they can now be seen shining on homes across the country.

The name itself is a misnomer: "Dutch" is a corruption of *Deutsch* (German), from the many persecuted German religious folk that settled in the land of William Penn, seeking freedom of worship. The "hex" was probably originally *sechs* (German for "six"). Since so many of these designs contain six-pointed stars, "sechs signs" became "hex signs." And so Pennsylvania Dutch hex signs are actually magical symbols that were originally created by persons of German origin, and are never used to hex. On the contrary; hex signs are tools of blessing, protection, health, and happiness.

It could possibly be that such symbols were originally religious in nature. If so, this was a form of religious magic. Symbols were painted onto barns asking for rain (when rain was needed for crops), or to guard against the intrusion of evil. People do still pray for rain and for protection.

Whatever their origins, whatever their original uses, hex signs are magical tools, and can be used by anyone.

There are many stories of the effectiveness of hex signs. People who've had signs painted for them swear that they've been instrumental in bringing rain in times of drought, conceiving children, patching up broken relationships, and all manner of magical changes.

Hex signs can only do these things, of course, if their users give them magical energy. How much more potent could they be if we actually made them ourselves?

And so, we have. To look at hex signs from the proper magical (though culturally incorrect) perspective, see them as magical symbols, created for a specific reason, and used with power.

We don't have the space to discuss every hex sign, but we've included a few illustrations so that you can actually see them. And we can discuss hex signs in a general way.

Meanings of Colors Used in Hex Signs

The colors used in creating hex signs are important, for color is a basic magical tool. Below are listed some of the colors and their basic meaning in "hex" magic (curiously enough, they almost exactly match European color magic):

Red: Love, protection, action, life, liberty

Yellow: Sacredness, deity, the sun, truth, children

Green: Fertility of the earth (which, to farmers, meant prosperity and security), good fortune, happiness, "luck"

Blue: Spirituality, protection, beauty

Violet: Power, humility, protection

Brown: The world, business, harvest, earthiness, sex

White: Purity, protection, joy

Black: Sex, black magic, sorcery

(Some of the magical meanings of these colors differ from the list given in part 3 of this book. It's best, however, to use the above correspondences when creating "hex" signs.)

Four-pointed star

Six-pointed star

Hex Sign Designs

The designs are as important as the colors. Below are some of the most common symbols found in hex signs, together with their traditional meanings:

Heart: Love

Goldfinch: Good fortune

Raindrops: Rain (what else?)

Rose: Peace, contentment

Oak leaves: Bodily strength

Five-pointed star: Protection, "good luck"

Six-pointed star: Love, protection

Eight-pointed star: Abundance, good will

Eight-pointed star

Double star (ten-pointed: The sun, light

Triple star (twenty-pointed): "Good luck," success, happiness, tulip, human's search for God, bliss in paradise

Heart, tulips

Creating a Six-Pointed Star Hex Sign

The six-pointed star (rosette) was probably the earliest form of structured hex sign ever created. It's still quite popular, and it happens to be the type of sign that we'll be describing here.

Items needed:

A red candle and holder
Paper
Compass (not the directional kind)
Pencil
A flat dish or a round piece of wood (6 inches or larger in
    diameter)
Red paint
White paint
Fine and medium paint brushes

You determine the size of your hex sign. Ideally, it should be about six inches in diameter. This is determined, in part, by the width that your compass can handle. (You remember the trusty old compass, don't you? It was that thing you always got for school and never used. A pencil is stuffed into one end, the pointed end is placed onto a piece of paper, and we then create a perfect circle by moving the pencil. Remember? Fine.)

It's best to practice drawing the rosette a few times before beginning the actual project. Using scratch paper, draw a circle with the compass and then, following the diagrams and instructions below, draw the rosette within it. The secret in creating a perfect rosette is to not alter the width of the compass in any way while making the rosette.

It's best to practice drawing the rosette several times until it's no longer necessary to refer to these instructions.

Each arc (of which there are six) is exactly one-half of the circle's width. For clarity's sake, here we'll be thinking of the circle as a clock. Twelve is straight up; three is to the right, six down, nine to the left. (The instructions may sound complicated, but the technique is quite simple.)

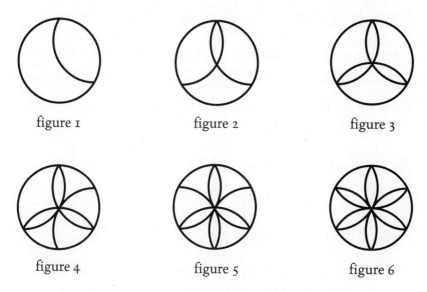

figure 1   figure 2   figure 3

figure 4   figure 5   figure 6

How to draw a six-pointed star

As you draw the design, visualize the symbol beaming out protective energy.

Step 1. Place the point of the compass in the center of the paper. Draw the outer circle (it should be at least six inches in diameter), but leave one-half inch or so of wood around the circle.

Step 2. Place the pointed tip of the compass onto the circle itself at two o'clock. Draw an arc across the circle. The middle of the arc should cross the center of the circle, and the ends should stop at twelve and four (see figure 1).

Step 3. Move the pointed tip of the compass to ten o'clock. Draw an arc from twelve to seven (figure 2).

Step 4. Move to six. Draw an arc from seven to four (figure 3).

Step 5. Move to four. Draw an arc from two to six (figure 4).

Step 6. Move to seven. Draw an arc from ten to six (figure 5).

Step 7. Move to twelve o'clock. Draw an arc from ten to two (figure 6). You've created your hex sign.

Step 8. Empower the red candle with protective energies. Light it and place it nearby while you work.

Step 9. You're now ready to paint. Paint the outer circle red.

Step 10. Carefully paint the rosette red.

Step 11. Paint the remainder of the inner circle white.

Allow the hex sign to dry beside the flaming red candle. Then, hang it up somewhere in the home with these words:

<blockquote>
I <i>place you with power.</i>
I <i>place you to guard this home.</i>
</blockquote>

It is done. (If you use waterproof paint, the protective hex sign can be attached to the exterior of your house.)

CHAPTER FOURTEEN

Spell Banners

BANNERS ARE MAGICAL objects. When hung outside on a breezy day, they move about as if by their own volition. Banners that bear magical symbols, and that have been created with power, are excellent magical tools.

No great European tradition of spell-banner use can be found. The Chinese, however, have long painted certain signs on banners of silk or paper and hung them to gain specific energies: wealth, long life, victory, and so on. Many such banners, of smaller size and housed in frames, can be seen hanging in places of Chinese business, and may be mistaken for purely decorative items. However, most invite money onto the premises.

Spell banners utilize the power of the element of air to release the energy that has been placed into them by the magician during their creation. They're quite simple to create, cost very little, and can be made for several purposes.

To Create the Spell Banner

Items needed:

A long, narrow sheet of paper at least 8½ x 22 inches
Water-based poster paints (green, blue, red, and black)
A fine paintbrush
Extra paper for practicing the designs
A bowl of pure water
A dish of salt
A candle (of the appropriate color; see below)
Incense and a censer

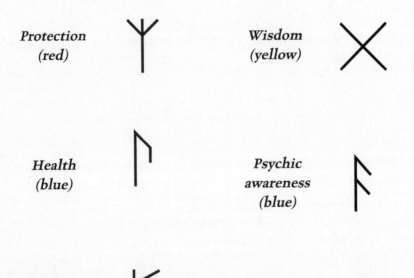

Protection
(red)

Wisdom
(yellow)

Health
(blue)

Psychic
awareness
(blue)

Money
(green)

Victory
(red)

Love
(red)

Decide upon your main magical need. Then, looking through the symbols included here, choose the one linked with your need.

If you can't find the appropriate symbol, notice the appropriate color paint. Black paint can be used for all needs.

Before actually creating your banner, practice painting the symbol several times. The symbols that we've chosen to be placed on our banners stem from ancient Norse alphabets (runes). They aren't difficult to paint, but keep these things in mind as you work:

- Create each stroke separately.
- Keep each line as straight as is possible.
- You're not merely painting symbols; you're creating manifesting energies, so create them with as great a degree of accuracy as is possible.

When you've selected your sign and can draw it with ease, place the bowl of salt to the north on your working area. Place the censer and incense to the east, the candle to the south, and the bowl of water to the west.

Light the candle. Light the incense. Place the sheet of paper in the midst of your working area. Set the bottle of paint and the brush nearby.

Touch the water with the forefinger of your protective hand and say, while sending purifying energy into it,

I exorcise this water of
all impurities
and uncleanliness.
Be pure and clean,
O creature of water.

Touch the salt and say, while sending purifying energy into it,

I bless this salt that it may serve me in my
magical working. Be pure and blessed.

Spell banner

Pick up the piece of paper. Sprinkle it with salt and say:

> I *consecrate you with earth.*

Wave it in the incense smoke. Say:

> I *consecrate you with air.*

Wave it through the candle's flame and say:

> I *consecrate you with fire.*

Moisten your fingers with the water, sprinkle it over the paper and say:

> I *consecrate you with water.*

Replace the paper on your working area.
Repeat this same consecration with the paint and paintbrush.

Now say the following, holding your hands palms downward over the assembled items:

You are no longer merely paper and ink;
you are vehicles of power.
May energy flow through you
and crystallize in this sign;
may the element of air release you
to speed my need to manifestation.
So mote it be.

Move the censer beside the dish of salt, the candle beside the censer, and the bowl of water beside the candle to clear your working area. Open the paint bottle.

Rouse energy within you. Strongly visualize. Take up the paint brush. Dip it into the paint. As you create the symbol or word, say these or similar words:

I paint with power.
The power of my need
plants the magic seed
in this hour.

As you paint, feel energy running from your hand, down through the brush, into the paint, and finally settling on the paper. Sense that this power is correctly focused on your magical need.

When you've finished painting, set down the brush and hold up the spell banner. Wave it gently over the salt, censer, candle, and water while saying:

Spell banner,
bring me _____.

Now hang the spell banner in an appropriate place in your bedroom, living room, on a patio, on the outside of your home (if it won't create curiosity), or even on a tree in a lonely forest.

Sit or stand before the spell banner for a few minutes. Stare into the symbol or word; realize that you've begun the process that will bring your need into manifestation.

Then leave the area. It has begun.

(If you hang the spell banner in a forest, leave the area, but return after a half hour. Retrieve it, guard it carefully at home, and hang it on the tree another time to further release its energy).

CHAPTER FIFTEEN

Spell Bottles

Spell bottles, also known as "Witch bottles," have been in use in England and the United States since at least the 1600s. Spell bottles were originally created to destroy the power of an evil magician or Witch thought to have cast a spell against the bottle's creator. They were often ceramic vessels, filled with hair, nails, and even the victim's urine. They were also walled up into new homes as magical guardians. Spell bottles of this type continued to be used well into the nineteenth century.

Spell bottles are apparently of English origin. Still, one example made from a glass wine bottle dated at 1740–1750 was found in Pennsylvania in 1976. And so, such protective devices certainly found their way from England to the United States with the colonists.

Spell bottles of the type described above are rarely if ever made today. Other forms, however, are still in use. These consist of a container, usually glass, filled with various objects of magical potency.

Spell bottles are made for a variety of purposes, and are used in numerous ways.

Some are hidden, while others are placed in windows of the home or in other prominent spots. All are concentrations of energy, created and empowered for specific magical purposes.

We'll be giving you instructions for making three spell bottles, but you can create many other types devoted to a multitude of magical needs. You could make a small spell bottle for your car, create and bury one in your garden for good growth, place one in a sickroom to speed the return of good health, and hang one near your pet's home. Using the tables at the end of this book will assist you in creating the magical "recipe" of your own spell bottles.

If, for some reason, your spell bottle is broken, simply create a new one.

Items needed to make a house protection spell bottle

House Protection Spell Bottle

Since the earliest spell bottles were created for protection, it seems fitting to begin with one made for this purpose. Ideally, such a bottle will be walled up in a new home under construction, or placed under the floorboards. If this is impossible, simply place it in a position of importance somewhere in the home.

Items needed:

> 1 glass jar with cork stopper or lid (a small canning jar is fine)
> 1 bowl
> ½ to 1 cup salt (depending on size of jar)
> 3 cloves garlic
> 9 bay leaves
> 7 tablespoons dried basil
> 4 tablespoons dill seeds
> 1 tablespoon sage
> 1 tablespoon anise
> 1 tablespoon black pepper
> 1 tablespoon fennel

In the morning, ideally on a bright and sunny day, assemble all items. Place the salt into the bowl and say:

> *Salt that protects, protect my home*
> *and all within it.*

Add the cloves of garlic to the bowl and say:

> *Garlic that protects, protect my home*
> *and all within it.*

Crumble the bay leaves, place in the bowl, and say:

> *Bay that protects, protect my home and all within it.*

Add the basil and say:

> *Basil that protects, protect my home*
> *and all within it.*

Add the dill and say:

> *Dill that protects, protect my home*
> *and all within it.*

Add the sage and say:

> *Sage that protects, protect my home and all within it.*

Add the anise and say:

> *Anise that protects, protect my home and all within it.*

Add the pepper and say:

> *Pepper that protects, protect my home*
> *and all within it.*

Add the fennel and say:

> *Fennel that protects, protect my home*
> *and all within it.*

Mix together the herbs and the salt with your hands. Through the movement of your hands and fingers, lend energy to the potent protective items. Visualize your home as a shining, safe, guarded, secure place of sanctuary.

Pour the mixture into the jar. Seal tightly and place in your home with the following words:

> *Salt and herbs, nine times nine*
> *Guard now this home of mine.*

It is done.

Money Spell Bottle

Items needed:

   5 old pennies
   5 dimes
   5 quarters (or, 5 each of 3 denominations of your country's
      coin currency, if outside the United States)
   5 kernels of dried corn
   5 kernels of dried wheat (or 5 teaspoons wheat flour)
   5 sesame seeds
   5 cinnamon sticks
   5 cloves
   5 whole allspice
   5 pecans

Place each item into a thin, tall bottle, such as a spice bottle. Cap it tightly. Shake the bottle with your projective hand for five minutes while chanting these or similar words:

> *Herbs and silver,*
> *copper and grain;*
> *work to increase*
> *my money gain.*

Place the money spell bottle on a table somewhere in your house. Leave your purse, pocketbook, wallet and/or checkbook near the bottle when at home. Allow money to come into your life.
   It is done.

A Love Spell Bottle

Items needed:

   Rose water (available in gourmet food stores, some markets,
      herb and health-food stores, or by mail)
   1 handful dried rose petals
   2 pinches dried lavender

Hold the rose petals between your palms. Empower them with love. Place in the bottle.

Hold the lavender between your palms. Empower them with love. Place in the bottle.

Fill the bottle with the rose water. Cap or cork. Hold the bottle between palms and press it against your chest, saying these or similar words:

Flowers drenched with love,
drench me with love.

Keep the love spell bottle in your bedroom.
It is done.

CHAPTER SIXTEEN

Flower Garlands

THROUGHOUT HISTORY AND around the globe, humans have used flowers and plants for personal decoration. In ancient Egypt, upper-class families held water-lily blossoms (inaccurately termed "lotuses") during banquets. Greek brides often tucked a sprig of blossoming hawthorn into their dresses. Olympic victors were crowned with laurel leaves. In parts of India, young brides placed garlands of flowers around their future mates' necks. In that same country, strings of chrysanthemums are worn for religious purposes. Sprigs of elder were worn in Europe to guard against evil.

Throughout Asia and the Pacific, flowers are often casually tucked behind an ear or twined around hats by both men and women, as a form of natural decoration. During the late 1960s and early 1970s in the United States, young people decorated both hair and beards with flowers. Even today, corsages and boutonnieres are given and worn, and the bride's bouquet is an integral part of most western-style marriages. The Tournament of Roses Parade held in Pasadena, California, seems to be a semi-sacred adoration of flowers.

Flowers have been strung into garlands for centuries, especially in Asia. They're used to adorn everything from oxcarts and altars to religious images and humans. But the liveliest and most intricate flower garlands have been, and continue to be, made on a string of islands in the Pacific Ocean.

Today, Hawaiian leis are a globally known symbol of love and welcome. Though leis have also been made of more durable materials (such as teeth, hair, nuts, seeds, and shells), the fragrant, fragile, and temporary flower lei is currently most popular.

Originally, few plant materials in Hawaii lent themselves for lei use. A few flowers, a few seed pods, some ferns, and a small number of other plants constituted the bulk of the materials. Soon, however, western explorers and eastern settlers brought dozens of new flowers and, with them, the raw materials to create a wide variety of new leis.

The most popular leis in Hawaii today—the plumeria, carnation, and orchid—are made from introduced, non-Hawaiian plants. No one really seems to mind, particularly the tourists who arrive and have these fragrant treasures placed around their necks.

By their very nature, decorative materials made of fresh flowers are ethereal creations to be enjoyed for a limited amount of time. Though we here in the west have usually associated them with ritual occasions or weddings, flower garlands can also be made for specific magical purposes. Though there isn't a long magical tradition regarding this practice, it's built upon some simple ideas.

First, plants—particularly fragrant flowers—possess earth powers. Making and wearing a garland releases these energies to its wearer far more effectively than would the same blooms placed in a distant, impersonal vase.

Additionally, the garland itself is a circle. Circles represent, among other things, perfection, completion, spirituality, and protection. Placing energy-possessing flowers in such a symbol around our necks intensifies their effects.

So, in this chapter, we'll describe a simple method of creating flower garlands. The unique rites that we present for use with these garlands are derived from the long history of ritualistic flower usage, contemporary Hawaiian leis, and plant magic in general.

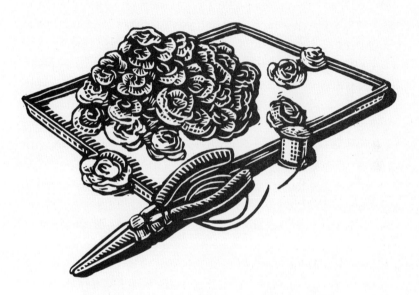

Items needed to make a love garland

A Love Garland

Items needed:

> 50 to 200 flowers*
> 1 12-inch piece strong (but thin) metal wire
> Needle nose pliers
> Strong cotton thread
> A large flat pan

*These should be sweetly scented flowers, such as rosebuds, tuberose, orange flowers, jasmine, and violet. Orchids can also be used, if they're available in large quantities. The number of flowers required for the project depends on the size of the blooms. This may seem to be an excessive number, but it really isn't. The larger the flower, the less you'll have to use.

First, gather or buy the flowers. Prepare them by separating them from their stems or branches. Place the flowers in the pan.

Make your needle from the wire. The wire should be stiff enough to hold its shape without flopping around. Straighten it so that it resembles a large needle. Next, using the pliers, fold over one end of the wire to create a small oval loop no larger than one-sixteenth of an inch—large enough so that thread can be passed through it, but narrow enough so that it can be passed through the flowers without causing damage. (In Hawaii, needles made specifically for stringing flowers are available. Here we're making a suitable substitute.) If necessary, reshape the wire. It should be as straight as possible.

Next, place your hands over the flowers and charge them with loving energies.

Thread the needle, but don't knot the thread. Trim the thread to a length of about thirty inches.

Carefully positioning the needle in the center of the flower, push it onto the needle and move it down toward the end. (Leave it at the end of the needle for now.)

Repeat with more flowers until the needle is full. When it is, carefully and gently push the strung flowers to the end of the string, allowing about two inches of the string's end to remain unflowered for tying.

Continue the entire process until about two inches of bare string remain on either end. The flowers must be pushed fairly tightly together or gaps will appear when the garland is worn.

Tie the ends together, saying:

I knot this garland
that love may bloom.

Hold the garland up to the north and say:

Love from the earth!

Hold up to the east and say:

> *Love from the air!*

Hold up to the south and say:

> *Love from the fire!*

Hold up to the west and say:

> *Love from the water!*

Slowly place it around your neck while saying and visualizing:

> *Garland of flowers,*
> *make love bloom.*

Sit for thirteen or more minutes visualizing the love that you'll soon share with another human being. Reinforce within you, if necessary, the fact that you deserve love.

When done, you can continue to wear the garland for the rest of the day. If this is impossible, charge a pink candle with love energies

Finished garland

and place the garland around it. Or, toss it into a lake, stream, river, or the ocean to further spread its energies.

Love will come to you.

A Protective Garland

Use carnations. Before stringing the flowers, remove the green calyx (base) of each flower and fluff the petals. Charge the flowers with protective energies.

String as directed above. When you've completed the garland, knot the two ends together, saying:

> This knot I tie;
> this knot I bind;
> I'm protected
> by this sign.

Place it around your neck. Wear it for at least half an hour. Protective rituals may be more potent while wearing this garland.

CHAPTER SEVENTEEN

A Prosperity Trivet

MANY THOUSANDS OF years ago, humans discovered that they could create pleasing patterns by pressing stones, twigs, and shells into muddy riverbanks. Such artworks were temporary, for rising water, rain, wind, and other natural forces would quickly sweep them away. Still, an idea was born: that of using small, flat objects to create larger pictures. Since virtually all ancient art was created for religious or spiritual purposes, these early pictures may have been offerings to the spirits of wind, water, and earth.

This art form, known today as mosaic, was refined and widely used in most of the great civilizations in creating religious scenes. Mosaics often graced temples and other religious structures and objects.

In ancient Sumer, buildings and walls were decorated by the placement of alternately colored cone-shaped bricks in patterns resembling mosaics. The Sumerians also created religious tools decorated with elaborate mosaics fashioned of shell, lapis lazuli, and carnelian.

The Greeks and Romans are renowned as the creators of huge, exquisitely detailed mosaic floors. These closely resemble what we today know as mosaics, for the Greeks were the first to cut marble of various colors into small pieces, which were then set into intricate patterns. The Romans learned the technique from the Greeks.

Both cultures lavishly decorated homes and temples with mosaics depicting religious scenes. In fact, the art of mosaic was so closely related to religion that the word probably derives from the Greek *mouseios,* "belonging to the Muses."

The Romans further refined the technique. They learned that volcanic ash mixed with water created a cement or grout that held the tiles in place. Thus, truly permanent mosaics could finally be created.

The Minoans were also mosaic makers. During one dig on Crete, archaeologists found a stone box. Inside were small *tesserae* (Latin for mosaic tiles) of quartz crystal, lapis lazuli, beryl, amethyst, and gold, ready to be used.

Mosaics weren't confined to the Old World. Peoples in Central America and Mexico crafted fine shields, statues, and religious objects covered with mosaic work. Tiles of jadeite, gold, colored shell, mother of pearl, coral, obsidian, and garnet were used in creating these works. One famous example is a representation of a skull completely covered with tiny jadeite tiles.

Throughout India and Thailand, temples and images of the Buddha are covered with mosaics. Among the materials used there are small mirrors, which make the whole structure (or object) shimmer as sunlight is reflected on the mirrored tiles.

Today, mosaics are made with small ceramic tiles. These materials are considerably less expensive than those used in the past, and allow a greater range of colors (and, thus, scenes) to be depicted. The early connection between mosaics and religion haven't been forgotten, as many churches in the United States are decorated with finely detailed mosaics, and stained glass is simply mosaic in another form.

This chapter explores the creation of a mosaic trivet designed to enhance prosperity. The square shape of the trivet represents earth, the element associated with money. The color green is also used in prosperity magic. Finally, the symbol created by the green tiles has long been wielded to increase finances. The completed project can be a powerful adjunct to prosperity rituals.

Items needed to make a mosaic trivet

Mosaic Trivet for Prosperity

Materials:

A square of wood, ½ inch thick, 9½ inches square
21 green 1-inch ceramic tiles
60 white 1-inch ceramic tiles
Permanent adhesive glue
Grout
Spatula

> Sponge
> Soft cloth
> Green candle
> Candle holder

Step 1. Mark the grid pattern (see illustration) on the wooden square. Each square is just a bit larger than 1 inch (extra width is for the grout). Mark squares that will contain white tiles with a W, green squares with a G.

Step 2. Put a dab of permanent adhesive glue on the back of one white tile and press it firmly on one wooden square. Center the tile in the square that you've drawn.

Step 3. Repeat with each tile. Work from right to left, the top row first, then each succeeding row.

Step 4. When all tiles have been placed, pour a small amount of grout into a clean bowl. Slowly add water and mix with a spatula until the grout resembles a creamy cake batter.

Step 5. Place a small amount of the grout on top of the tiles. Spread it evenly over the tiles with the spatula or with your fingers until all crevices between the tiles have been filled.

Step 6. Wipe off excess grout from the tiles with a lightly moistened sponge, leaving a clean surface.

Step 7. Buff the trivet with a soft cloth to a shiny gloss.

Step 8. Allow to dry, undisturbed, for twenty-four hours to three days.

Step 9. To use your prosperity trivet to bring needed cash to your home, begin on the night of the New Moon. Place a crisp one-dollar bill on the center of the trivet. Surround this with four silver coins (preferably solid silver). Empower a green candle with money attracting energies and place it in its holder. Place the candle on top of the dollar bill, on top of the trivet. Light the candle, hold your hands over the assembled objects, and say these or similar words:

> Powers of earth,
> powers of rune;
> move on this night
> of the New Moon.
> Carefully crafted
> symbol in green:
> bring me more money
> than what's here seen.
> I call the earth
> to bind my spell;
> what's here begun
> will finish well.

Completed mosaic trivet for prosperity

Allow the candle to flame for twenty minutes. Snuff the flame and repeat each night for six more nights.

(When not in use, the trivet can be hung on a wall to continuously attract money to your home.)

CHAPTER EIGHTEEN

Spell Potpourri

AROMATIC MIXTURES OF herbs have been created in many lands throughout recorded history. Fragrant flowers, simple herbs, and rare spices were mixed and used for purposes both magical and medicinal.

Mixtures that could be considered to be the forerunners of potpourri were made in ancient Egypt, Greece, and Rome, but it wasn't until the Renaissance that the art of creating what we know as *potpourri* reached its zenith. Potpourri and other fragrant mixtures were rarely made for magical purposes, for the magic of herbs had been largely forgotten.

During these times, bathing was out of vogue and sewers were unknown. Windows were few and allowed little air to circulate in the house. Under these conditions, it isn't surprising that fragrant herbs were called upon to brighten everyday life with their delightful scents.

The poor and the rich alike devised several ingenious methods to use fragrant flowers and herbs to perfume themselves and their homes. Those with money had far greater options, for traders would bring rare and costly spices from overseas. Soon scent rings, pomanders, tussymussies, and sachets were made and carried to sweeten the air. Incense was burned. Sweet herbs were strewn onto rugs to release their fragrances when trod upon, and sachets were tied onto chairs, couches, and beds.

Potpourri was also used to clear the air. These were mixtures of either fresh or dried herbs, flowers, and spices that were kept in fast-lidded jars. To release the fragrance, the box or jar was opened, allowing the aroma to mask baleful odors, making the home a much more pleasant place to live.

Some of these herbs were also thought to contain healthful qualities, and so were used to prevent the spread of disease, but the Witchcraft and heresy trials had done much to make the populace forget the magical qualities of herbs. Thus, potpourri were viewed as either pleasantly scented mixtures or as weapons in the arsenal against disease—not as tools of magic.

Today, our knowledge of the subtle powers of plants allows us to create potpourris designed to produce specific magical results. As usual, visualization is a vital part of this process. The power of the potpourri rides on its scent.

Finding the Ingredients

Many flowers and herbs can be found in gardens or in wild places. For those not immediately available, try local herb shops, health, or occult stores. Many are available in supermarkets and gourmet shops. If you still can't find the ingredients, write to the herb suppliers listed in the appendix for mail-order delivery (or see the list of herbal substitutions included in part 3).

If you wish to collect and dry at least some of the ingredients of your potpourri, pick them in the morning, after the dew has dried from them. Lay the flowers or herbs on trays, out of direct sunlight, preferably in a place with good air circulation.

Allow the plant materials to dry for at least ten days (longer, if the weather is cold). The flowers or herbs must be completely, absolutely dry, or mold will develop within the potpourri. Once they're dried, you're ready to begin.

Storing the Potpourri

Potpourri are usually kept in closed boxes or jars. The lid is lifted to release the scent. Any type of jar or box with a tight-fitting lid is suitable.

Special potpourri containers, made of ceramic and perforated with holes, are available in some specialty stores. These continuously release the mixture's fragrance, and, of course, the power. Such containers (or others, such as an open jar, or even a large seashell) are fine for long-term mixtures, such as those designed to attract money, to protect the home, and to attract love and health.

Alternately, simply tie the potpourri into a small bag. Again, the power is steadily released.

Using the Potpourri

A potpourri's power is released within its scent. Thus, smelling a potpourri is actually an act of magic, for we're moving the energy contained within the mixture into ourselves. We release the potpourri's fragrance only when we need its energies.

If you've placed the potpourri into a closed box or jar, breathe deeply for a few moments. Visualize your need (if you've made a money potpourri, the need is obviously money). Open the box or jar.

Inhale. Breathe deeply. Feel the energy flowing into your body, creating real changes. Continue to visualize. Allow the potpourri to affect you. Repeat as many times a day as you see fit.

If you've placed the potpourri in an open container, run your fingers through the mixture at least once a day. Bend and smell the evocative scent several times a day.

This is a subtle form of magic. The effects of the potpourri will be subtle as well, but they will occur if you've correctly mixed and used them. Open yourself to change, and change will manifest.

Replacing the Potpourri

Magical potpourri kept in open containers should be replaced every three months, or when their fragrances dwindle. Bury the spent potpourri in the earth and create a new one, if necessary.

Potpourri kept in closed containers can last indefinitely. Indeed, some potpourri are still fragrant twenty years after their preparation. You shouldn't have to replace them.

Mixing the Potpourri

Technically, this is quite simple. Magically, this is the most important step.

Step 1. Gather the necessary ingredients. (All ingredients should be completely dried. Don't substitute an oil for an herb unless recommended.)

Step 2. Place the first ingredient into a large bowl. Touch it. Stroke it. Smell its aroma, visualize.

Step 3. Separately add each ingredient following the same system: touch, smell, visualize.

Step 4. Rub together the herbs with your fingers, mingling their powers and fragrances. Deepen your visualization. Feel the power under your fingertips. Sense its realness.

Step 5. Place the potpourri in a suitable container and use as needed.

That said, here are the recipes. Though we list recommended quantities, feel free to alter these to suit your individual taste.

Items needed to make potpourri

Money Potpourri

    1 cup oakmoss
    1 cup cedar shavings
    1 cup patchouly
    ¼ cup vetivert, powdered (or pulled apart)
    1 tablespoon nutmeg, ground
    1 teaspoon cinnamon, ground
    1 pinch ginger, ground

Protection Potpourri

    ½ cup juniper berries, whole
    ½ cup basil, whole
    2 tablespoons frankincense, ground
    2 tablespoons dill seeds, whole
    2 tablespoons fennel seeds, whole
    2 tablespoons clove, whole
    8 bay leaves, torn to pieces

Love Potpourri

1½ cups rose petals or rose buds
I cup lavender
¼ cup camomile
¼ vanilla bean, chopped (optional)
2 tablespoons calamus or benzoin, ground
2 tablespoons cardamom seed, ground

Psychic Potpourri

I cup lemongrass
½ cup mugwort
¼ cup star anise (or regular anise), whole
2 tablespoons thyme
2 tablespoons yarrow
I teaspoon mace
Dash genuine saffron (if available)

Healing Potpourri

I cup rosemary, whole
¼ cup coriander seed, whole
¼ cup sandalwood, ground or chips
⅛ cup sassafras, whole
2 tablespoons peppermint
I pinch poppy seed

Courage Potpourri

½ cup black pepper berries, whole (not ground)
½ cup allspice berries, whole
⅛ cup thyme

CHAPTER NINETEEN

A Magic Mirror

MIRRORS AND REFLECTIVE surfaces have always been used as tools to promote psychic awareness.* Originally, mirrors fashioned of polished metal or volcanic glass served as a focal point for the seer. Bowls filled with darkened liquid, and even pools of ink, were also used. The idea was consistent: gazing at a reflective surface drowsed the conscious mind and awakened psychic awareness.

Surprisingly, the familiar glass mirror as we know it today has been little used in promoting psychic awareness since it's creation in the sixteenth century. This is due, in part, to the fact that the mirror's near perfect reflection distracts the conscious mind, which easily (and usually) inhibits psychic awareness.

If, however, we situate the mirror so that it reflects a blank image, and use it in a darkened room, even these mirrors can be

---

*For more magical mirror lore, see Cunningham and Harrington's *The Magical Household*.

extremely helpful in contacting the psychic mind. This is the type of mirror that we'll be making.

One wind-swept day, we walked along a beach. A recent storm had covered the sand with literally hundreds of shells of every description. We collected them and wondered what we could do with them.

The answer came quite easily: why not make a magic mirror bordered with shells? Shells are evocative of the ocean, and the ocean is a powerhouse of psychic energy. Thus, this project was born.

Psychic awareness is our birthright as human beings. With tools such as this, we can recapture this innate ability and use it to better our lives.

Items needed to make a magic mirror

Making a Magic Mirror

Items needed:

> 50 to 150 shells of various sizes. Scallop shells are ideal for this project. Have at least one dozen tiny shells, which you'll use to fill in small spaces. Many craft stores carry shells. Check your phone book or the nearest beach. (Beach-gathered shells are best, but use what you can find.)
>
> Clean sand or white-colored, fine aquarium gravel
>
> Household glue. This shouldn't be instant drying, and should dry clear.
>
> An 8-inch square piece of thin wood or corrugated cardboard (wood is preferable, but thick, corrugated cardboard will do in a pinch)
>
> 1 round, 4-inch mirror. These are available almost everywhere. If necessary, dismantle a small makeup mirror. The mirror should have no molding or frame. If it does, remove it. (If you decide to use a larger or smaller mirror, adjust the size of the wooden [or cardboard] base proportionately: the base should be about twice the width of the mirror.)
>
> A ruler and pencil
>
> Moistened and dry cotton cloth
>
> A large scrap piece of corrugated cardboard
>
> A chewed piece of bubble gum or a piece of tape
>
> 1 blue candle and candle holder. This will be used in the ritual to bless the magic mirror.

Step 1. Assemble all the items on a table or other flat working surface. Sort the shells according to size and, if you wish, color. Hold your hands over the shells and say:

> *Spiraled treasures of the sea,*
> *awake the psychic mind in me.*

Step 2. Using the pencil and ruler, draw lines across the wooden or cardboard base, from A to C, and from B to D. This will allow you to accurately place the mirror onto the center of the base.

Step 3. Allow at least one-half hour for this step. Place the mirror onto the center of the base, using the lines as a guide. Now place the shells in a symmetrical pattern on the base around the mirror. Some of them may overlap a bit onto the mirror itself. Some suggestions: begin with the largest shells first, then fit in the smaller ones. Large shells can be placed at the base's four corners. Shells of different colors can be alternated to form pleasing, contrasting patterns. A large shell can be placed between two corners to create the "top" of the mirror. Cover as much of the base as possible. If you don't like the pattern that you've created, begin again. This is the time to decide, not later when you're actually gluing the shells in place.

Step 4. When you've finalized your pattern, individually transfer the shells to a flat surface, recreating the same pattern there.

Step 5. Enchant the mirror by holding your hands above it and saying, in a soft, dreamy voice:

> *Glow, mirror,*
> *shimmer with power.*
> *Assist me in my workings.*

Step 6. Apply household glue to the back of the mirror. Also apply glue to the center of the base. Place the mirror onto the center of the base. Press base and mirror firmly together. Allow to dry for at least one-half hour.

Step 7. Apply glue to the base around the mirror. (If glue smears on the mirror, remove it with a moistened piece of cloth). Spread glue evenly with a finger. Pour the sand onto the glue, ensuring an even coat. Allow to dry for at least fifteen minutes.

Step 8. Tip up one end of the base and tap gently on the reverse side. Some sand will slide off. If the base isn't completely covered with sand, reglue those areas and pour on more sand. Let dry for fifteen minutes.

Step 9. Spread household glue onto the scrap piece of cardboard (or a paper plate). Press the bubble gum or a piece of tape onto the center of one large shell that you'll be using in your pattern. Using the gum as a holder, lift the shell, quickly dip its edges into the glue, and press it firmly oto the base according to your previously created pattern. Carefully detach the gum or tape.

Step 10. Repeat this entire procedure for each shell. Begin with the largest shells. It's best to also start with those shells that are close to the mirror, then work your way outward toward the edges of the base. Remove all glue smears immediately from the mirror with a moist cloth and dry.

Don't be tempted to check if the glue has fastened the shells to the mirror. It's best not to touch them until the glue has had time to dry.

If you find that you're losing the pattern that you've created, alter it as best as you can. Shells seem to grow or shrink when you're actually trying to glue them to fit the design.

Step 11. Fill in any holes with leftover small shells. These can be difficult to accurately place, so use care. Allow the glue to dry for at least a one-half hour.

Step 12. Gently touch each shell. If any are loose, reglue and allow to dry for at least fifteen minutes.

Step 13. Charge the blue candle with psychic energy. Place it into the holder. Place holder onto the center of the mirror. Say these or similar words with your hands held palms downward over the mirror:

Candle lights
mirror bright:
bring to me
the second sight.

Allow the candle to burn for nine, eighteen, twenty-seven, or thirty-six minutes. Snuff out the candle's flame and wrap the mirror in blue cloth when not in use.

To use, position the mirror so that it reflects the ceiling (this may be achieved by leaning it against a book). Turn off the lights. Empower a blue candle, light it, and place it behind the mirror (where it won't be reflected). Sit comfortably before the mirror, breathe deeply, and gaze into the mirror. Allow yourself to be psychic.

Completed magic mirror

CHAPTER TWENTY

Spell Boxes

BOXES ARE ONE of the simplest and most basic of tools. Surely they can't be possessed of magic, some might think. Why, millions of boxes have been created, out of every type of material, to store and to contain goods—from jewelry to hats to cereal. What could be mystical about such everyday objects?

Many things. Those handy with geometry and scissors can create a box from a single piece of cardboard or paper. Thus, the artist has transformed a flat object into a square or rectangular (or even round) object. As we're fond of saying, transformation is the definition of magic.

Though the creation of the box is a type of magical art, it's what we do with it that determines its magical uses. Boxes, after all, are used to contain. Throughout history, boxes have stored both household goods and magical objects, to protect them from dust as well as contamination. It is this quality of boxes—containment—that is used in magic.

Materials to make spell boxes

The story of Pandora's box (from classical mythology) is a negative example of the way in which energies can be stored in boxes—and of how they can be released. Similar stories, often of a more positive nature, can be discovered in other cultures from other times.

In ancient Egypt, ceremonial objects used to dress the statues of the gods in temple rites were kept in boxes known as *menet*, which were surmounted by four ostrich feathers. The Iroquois kept ritual regalia in boxes made of birch. Many Renaissance spells instruct us to place certain objects into boxes. And even today, hope chests are often filled with wishes for a happy marriage, as well as with linens put away for that future day.

Magically, the box is linked with the number four (for the four corners of any one face). Four is the number of the elements (powerhouses of magic) and so this symbolism is clear: the box contains the essence of all types of change.

Keep in mind this information, and forget everything you've ever heard about Pandora's box. These spell boxes are designed for positive uses.

The Box Itself

The spell box should be of wood and fairly small, about six inches in diameter. It should have a lid that fits tightly, hinged or not. Ideally, create your own box from wood. If you're not handy in this department, choose any other wooden box. (Old wooden cigar boxes will do, but sand off the label.) Many plain wooden boxes are available at craft stores. For best results, leave the box undecorated.

If you're a carpenter, feel free to design and create your own boxes.

Preparing the Box for Magic

On the night of the Full Moon, raise the box's lid. Hold up the box to the north and say these words:

> *By the powers of the earth . . .*

Face east and say:

> *By the powers of the air . . .*

Face south and say:

> *By the powers of fire . . .*

Face west and say:

> *By the powers of water . . .*

Return to the north and say:

I empower this spell box.
You are now a tool of magic.
Assist me in my transformations!

The box is now ready for use in spells of all types. When not in use, wrap the box in plain, white cotton cloth and store out of sight.

The spell box should only be used for one rite at a time, but it can be utilized for any possible positive magical change. Though we've given you some ideas below, feel free to improvise and create your own spell box rites.

For example, you might place rosebuds and your wedding picture into the box if you're having a touch of relationship problems. Or, write your secret wish on a piece of paper and place it in the box with appropriate herbs or stones (see tables). A third example: store your tarot cards in a special spell box made just for this purpose. With the cards, place herbs that promote psychic awareness (such as psychic potpourri; see chapter 18).

Spell boxes are curiously powerful things. We place charged materials into them. The box then mixes and merges these energies, but traps them within its confines. Only when the lid is lifted can they escape and do their work.

Below are some examples of how to use the spell box. Feel free to create your own versions.

The same spell box can be used for many magical purposes.

The Job Spell Box

Items needed:

Your spell box
1 to 2 tablespoons dried patchouly, fern, or vervain (in a small bowl)
2 to 4 tablespoons salt, fresh earth, or sand

1 plate
4 small polished tiger's-eye, aventurine, or peridot stones
1 green candle
1 candle holder

Hold the spell box in your hands. Send power into it. Visualize yourself working that job and say these or similar words:

> *Powers and energies,*
> *mingle and merge.*
> *Bring me the job*
> *that I deserve.*

Put down the box. Empower the herb by touching it with your fingertips while visualizing, and by saying:

> I *charge you to be a vehicle of manifestation.*
> *Manifest my perfect job!*

Sprinkle the charged herb into the box.

Next, sprinkle the salt, fresh earth, or sand onto a plate. With the index finger of your projective hand, trace this symbol into the substance.

Draw with power. After a few moments, carefully pour the charged sand, earth, or salt into the box.

Hold one of the stones in your hand. Empower it and place into the box. Repeat with the remaining stones.

Hold your palms downward over the filled spell box. Renew your visualization's power. Say these or similar words:

> *Powers and energies*
> *mingle and merge.*
> *Bring me the job*
> *that I deserve.*

Empower the candle, place it into its holder. Close the spell box's lid. Light the candle and burn before the spell box for thirteen minutes. Quench its flame.

Leave the box undisturbed for twenty-four hours. The next night, burn the candle again for thirteen minutes in front of the spell box.

On the third night, light the candle once again, saying these words:

> *Powers swirling in this box:*
> *fly away now, strong and free!*
> *Bring to me the job I need!*
> *This is my will, so mote it be!*

Raise (or remove) the box's lid, releasing the energies that have grown within it. Feel the power shooting forth from the box to bring your need into manifestation.

After a few moments, leave the area. Let the candle burn for thirteen minutes. Snuff out the candle and close the box.

Each night thereafter, open the spell box and repeat the above chant while burning the candle for thirteen minutes until it has been consumed.

Afterward, bury the spell box's contents in the earth. It is done.

The Love Spell Box

This rite is designed to attract a nonspecific person into your life. It cannot be used to attract a specific person. (Remember: to attract love, you must first love yourself.)

Items needed:

Your spell box
1 small piece paper
1 pencil
1 pair scissors
¼ cup dried rose petals
¼ cup dried lavender flowers
2 polished rose quartz stones

  1 small ring of some kind, preferably silver or copper, pur-
     chased for this purpose only (old friendship, wedding, or
     relationship rings should not be used)
  1 pink candle
  1 candle holder

Using the scissors, cut the paper into a heart shape small
enough to fit into your spell box without folding it.

Visualize. On the heart-shaped piece of paper, draw the magical
symbol for love:

Draw with power. When finished, place the "valentine" into
your spell box.

Next, empower the rose petals with love. Place them in the
spell box. Empower the lavender flowers with love and add to the
spell box.

Charge the rose quartz stones with love and add to the box.

Place the ring between the palms of your hands and hold them
over the spell box while saying:

Symbol of love,
Send me love.

Gently place the ring into the box.

Charge the pink candle with love. Place in its holder. Close the
spell box's lid.

Light the candle and let it burn for thirteen minutes before
your spell box, then quench its flames. Close the box again.

Leave the spell box undisturbed for twenty-four hours. On the
second night, open the box, burn the candle for thirteen minutes
once again, then quench the candle, and close the box.

On the third night, light the candle but don't open the box. Say
these or similar words:

Petals, lavender, quartz, and ring
the blessings of love you now bring.
Send your power speeding away;
this is my will; this is the way.

Open your spell box and sense its energies spiralling into the sky to bring your love into manifestation.

Let the candle burn for thirteen minutes, then quench its flame. Close the spell box.

Open the love spell box and burn the candle for thirteen minutes each night. Close the spell box when not in use.

When the candle is gone, bury the contents of the spell box, but retrieve the ring and keep in a safe place. It is done.

A Psychic Spell Box

This spell box differs from the others presented above. It's made in the same way, but is opened only when you wish to contact your psychic mind. It's well known that psychic awareness isn't a gift that only special people possess. We can all be psychic, through study and practice. This psychic spell box can be a tool to assist in this devotion.

This spell box is best created and used at night.

Items needed:

Your spell box
1 large bowl
¼ cup lemongrass
1 teaspoon whole cloves
1 teaspoon nutmeg, ground
1 teaspoon orange peel, dried
3 small polished amethysts
1 small polished aquamarine
1 small polished citrine
1 small quartz crystal
1 small bottle containing pure spring (or well) water, tightly lidded or capped
1 blue candle
1 candle holder

Begin by placing the lemongrass into the bowl. Touch it with your fingers. Relax. Breathe deeply and run your fingers through the herb, visualizing yourself as a psychic person. Relax and send soothing psychic energy into the herb.

Add the cloves and mix with the lemongrass, continuing to visualize. Add separately the nutmeg and orange peel, mixing them with the previously added herbs. Pour the mixed herbs into your spell box while saying:

> *Herb and seed and flower,*
> *Give me psychic power.*

Next, hold the three amethysts between the palms of your hands until they become warm, charging them with your visualization. Gently place them in the box.

Repeat with the aquamarine, the citrine, and the quartz crystal, adding each to the box. After putting the quartz crystal into your spell box, say these or like words:

> *Moon light,*
> *moon bright,*
> *waterfalls of trembling white:*
> *mirrors of the unseen world*
> *are unveiled in my sight.*

Finally, hold the small bottle of water between your palms and feel its cool, soothing psychic energy. Place it into the spell box with these or similar words:

> *Dew and rain, fog and sea,*
> *awaken psychic energy:*
> *this is my will, so mote it be.*

Charge the blue candle. Place into its holder and burn for nine minutes before the spell box (do not yet close its lid).

Close the lid of the spell box, then snuff out the candle's flame. Burn the candle before the spell box every day for nine minutes until the candle is gone (closing the spell box between sessions).

Whenever you have need of the box, even before the candle is gone, light the blue candle (or any other blue candle, if the original candle has burned itself out), open the box, and slowly say these or similar words:

Conscious mind . . .
is now blind . . .
psychic mind . . .
is now mine . . .

Use as needed, especially in conjunction with the use of tarot cards, crystals, rune stones, or other psychic tools.

CHAPTER TWENTY ONE

The Powers of Wheat

NO ONE CAN say with certainty when or how it began. Perhaps some farmer, bending to scythe the last bunch of ripe wheat or oats at the end of the harvest, gathered it up in his or her hand and sensed that this was a link with the fertility of the earth; a mystical summation of the provider of abundance and prosperity.

Wheat sustained life. It was a product of the rich soil below, the sun above, and of gentle rain. It was a gift from the agricultural deities.

And so early farmers began reverencing the earth with a ritual of sacrifice and thanksgiving by creating a figure of the harvest maiden or the Corn Mother. These were created by plaiting (a process similar to braiding) wheat stalks into beautiful shapes. The first of these were probably female shapes; later, the range of designs widely varied.

Such "corn dollies" (the term "dolly" is apparently derived, in this instance, from "idol") were constructed and used throughout Britain, in France, Greece, Poland, Asia, and elsewhere. The techniques and materials used to create these images varied, but the ritual purpose behind them was constant: celebrating abundance and praying that it would last until the following year, at which time another corn dolly would be made. Corn dollies aren't made of corn. In Britain, the word "corn" is used to describe all grains except maize. Thus, corn dollies are made of wheat, barley, oats, and other grains.

This is a challenging craft. The art of wheat-weaving requires full concentration and attention to technique. Infinite patience is necessary when first learning this craft. However, the weaver is rewarded with wonderfully magical objects that links us with our ancestors who planted and reaped and rejoiced in the powers of the earth.

The Materials

To make corn dollies, you'll need a large supply of hollow-stemmed wheat. Many modern wheat hybrids are solid stemmed, so search for the hollow varieties. Some craft stores and florists sell wheat stalks, particularly in the fall. (Mail-order sources for wheat stalks can be found in the appendix.)

Tools

For all projects listed here, you'll need scissors and deep-yellow thread.

Preparing the Wheat

Use only the upper portion of each stalk, from the seed head to the joint where the highest leaf juts out from the stalk. With a pair of scissors, cut off the stalk just above the topmost joint. Do this with every stalk and discard the lower portions of each stalk.

Cut above the topmost joint

Now that they're "clean," divide the wheat stalks according to width (not length). You might start out with three piles: small, medium, and large. Then subdivide these even further until most of the straws are bunched with others of nearly the same width. Doing this saves much time during the actual plaiting process.

If you use green wheat you're ready to begin. If, as is more probable, the wheat is dried, soak it in warm water for about a half hour. This softens the stalks so that they can be easily bent. Soaking them for too long, however, will make them split during plaiting.

While the wheat is soaking, gather together the specific materials necessary for the project.

After the wheat is pliant, remove it from the water and place it in a damp towel.

You're ready to begin.

Circles of Power
(Three-Straw Plait)

These simple projects are also known as countryman's favors. They were once quickly fashioned right in the field and given to loved ones. Here, however, the plait is fashioned into a protective charm for the home.

As you weave (according to the instructions below), visualize your home as a fortress of protective energy into which negativity and evil cannot enter. Even though you may be struggling with the wheat and these directions, as simple as they seem, hold this picture of your home within your mind. If you wish, place a photograph of your house in a place where you can look at it during the plaiting.

Three-straw plait

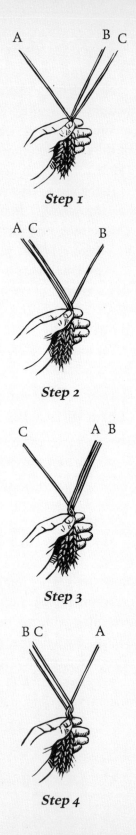

Items needed:

> 3 wheat straws
> Scissors
> Yellow thread
> Bright red ribbon or yarn

Step 1. Hold three straws and tie them tightly with yellow thread just below the heads. Hold the straws in your left hand (if right-handed). Hold straws B and C (see step 1) together, bending them away from straw A. Keep the knot firmly between your first finger and thumb.

Step 2. Bend straw C toward you and lay it over straw B so that it is next to straw A. Use your thumb to firmly bend the wheat.

Step 3. Bend straw A toward you over straw C and lay it beside straw B

Step 4. Bend straw B toward you over straw A and lay it beside straw C.

Step 5. Repeat steps 1 through 4 many times. The simple weave will begin to build up. Bend the straws tightly so that gaps don't show in the weave.

Step 1

Step 2

Step 3

Step 4

Step 6. When the plait is about seven inches long, tie off the end with strong yellow thread. Tie the two ends of the plait together to form a circle, while saying:

> *I knot you for protection.*

Set aside the first circle of power.

Step 7. Make another seven-inch length of three-straw plait, following steps 1–5 above. When it's finished, place one end through the first wheat circle and tightly tie together the ends. The two circles will interlock (like a chain). As you tie, say:

> *I knot you for protection.*

Step 8. Make one more seven-inch length and tie the ends together through the second circle, saying:

> *I knot you for protection.*

Step 9. Hang the circles of power up to dry. When the straw is once again brittle, cover the lowest join (where the circles touch; see page 157) with a bow of bright red ribbon or yarn. As you knot the first bow, say something like the following while visualizing your home as a place of protection and safety:

> *Golden wheat,*
> *circles of power,*
> *guard this household*
> *from this hour.*

Step 10. Repeat step 9 with the additional two plaited wheat circles, repeating your words and visualization.

Step 11. Prominently hang the charm in your home. Do this with power. It will guard your house from all manner of ills.

Health Corn Dolly (Five-Straw Plait)

This project is a variation of the technique used for the circles of power above. This more ambitious corn dolly requires five straws which, when plaited, produce a much wider dolly.

You'll need:

> 30 to 40 wheat straws
> Scissors
> Yellow thread
> A small piece of blue cotton fabric
> Blue thread or yarn
> Blue ribbon (or yarn)
> 1 teaspoon of mixed health herbs (any of the following can be used, in any combination: dried carnation petals, rose petals, coriander, juniper, marjoram, sage, cedar, nutmeg, sassafras, thyme)

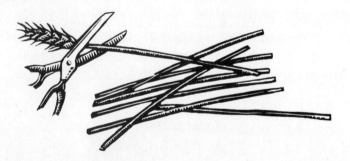

Cutting off the wheat head

Joining Straws

Because more wheat is used in this project, you'll find that the straws won't be large enough to complete it. Straws may also split. When this happens, it's necessary to join a new straw to the old one.

First, cut off the wheat head from the new straw. Snip off the end of the old straw to the last "corner," where it is covered by another straw. Gently push the thin end of the new straw into the "old" one and simply continue building up the dolly.

Choosing a straw that is of a slightly smaller width facilitates this process.

Joining straws

Now, to the health corn dolly. During its construction, visualize health and healing. Even as you struggle with the wheat and with the directions, remember your ritual intent.

Step 1. Mix the ground, dried herbs and spices in a small bowl with your fingers. As you mix them, visualize health energy flowing into the herbs. Feel them tingling under your fingertips, vibrating with energy.

Step 2. Place one teaspoon of the mixed, empowered herbs on the center of the small piece of blue cloth.

Step 3. With blue thread or yarn, tie the ends of the cloth tightly together, trapping the herbs inside the cloth. Trim off any excess cloth with the scissors.

Step 3

Step 4. Hold the fragrant bundle in your projective hand. Gently squeeze it. Sense the energies within it. Set it aside.

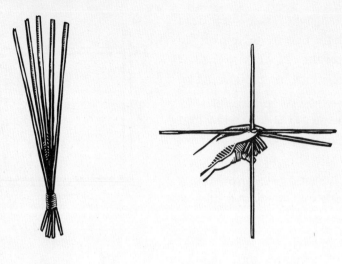

Step 5   **Step 6**

Step 5. Tie together five straws of the same width just below the heads. Cut off the heads.

Step 6. Hold the five straws as in the illustration above. Separate them so that one straw faces north, two east, one south, and one west. The straw ends and the knot that binds them should be toward you, not away from you. Hold the knot between the thumb and the first finger of the projective hand.

Step 7. Bend the upper east straw under the lower east straw and then over it, laying it directly beside the north straw.

Step 8. Turn the whole arrangement one-quarter turn clockwise, so that two straws are again in the east.

Step 7

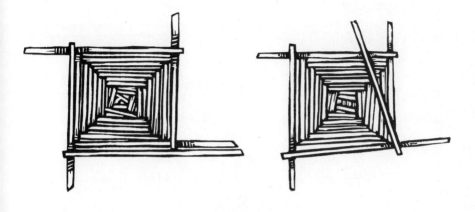

Step 9

Step 9. Repeat steps 7 and 8 several times. Make each bend tight. The dolly will gradually build up toward you as the straws are bent.

Step 10. Add new straws as the old ones grow too short. Thick straws seem to split more readily than thinner ones. Simply insert fresh straws.

Step 11. When the dolly is large enough to contain the herb bundle, squeeze the trapped herbs inside it and gently push it into the dolly.

Step 12. Begin decreasing the size of the dolly over the herb bundle: with the straws in the usual position (i.e., two to the east), bend the upper east straw under and then over the lower east straw, and lay it to the left of the north straw.

Step 13. Turn the project clockwise.

Step 14. Repeat steps 12 and 13 several times. The dolly ends will gradually decrease in size until it's too small to weave. At this point, tie together the straw ends with yellow thread.

Step 15. Snip off the excess straw ends one-half inch above the knot.

Step 16. Tie a bow of blue ribbon or yarn around the straws to hide the thread, leaving a large loop for hanging purposes.

Completed health dolly

Step 17. Hold the completed health dolly gently in your hands. Visualize it maintaining your health.

Step 18. Hang the dolly in your bedroom. This corn dolly can be made without herbs as a simple household charm to promote abundance and prosperity. Alternately, herbs can be empowered, bundled, and placed into the dolly for a number of other magical needs. (Part 3 lists herbs and colors appropriate for specific magical needs.)

Corn dollies aren't easy to make. They're challenging. But these are direct links with long-gone peoples who lived in harmony with the earth, and who revered her.

If you try these (and we hope you do), persevere. Work with the wheat, not against it, and your efforts will soon glow from walls and bedposts and chimneys.

Invoke the powers of wheat!

part three
the tables

Colors, Shells, Herbs, Stones, Feathers, and Woods

THESE MAGICAL TABLES of correspondences are for use in creating your own spell crafts. These simple lists can be utilized to create powerful ritual objects of many kinds for a variety of magical goals.

Colors

Colors are uniquely powerful symbols. In magic, they also contain power that can be of use during ritual.

There are many systems linking colors with specific magical energies. The following is a compilation of different traditions, including American folk magic and some other traditions. (For more color magic information, see chapter 13, "A Protective Hex Sign," and the below list of feathers.)

Use the below list when choosing cloth, paints, clays, sands, candles, and other tools for creating your own spell crafts.

Red: Maintaining health, strength, physical energy, sex, passion, courage, protection. Widely used in defensive magic. The color of the element of fire. Red is associated with blood (and thus, life and death), birth, volcanoes, and intense emotions. The Zuni of America linked this color with the south. Throughout Polynesia, red was a sacred color associated with both the deities and with the highest social classes

Pink: Love, friendship, compassion, relaxation. Pink is symbolic of gentle emotions and of emotional unions. It's less intense than red

Orange: General attraction, energy. Orange is a lesser aspect of red

Yellow: Intellect, confidence, divination, communication, eloquence, travel, movement. Yellow is the color of the element of air. It symbolizes the sun, grain, and the power of thought. To the Zuni, it symbolized the north. In Polynesia, yellow was a color of royalty and divinity

Green: Honey, prosperity, employment, fertility, healing, growth. Green is the color of the element of earth and symbolizes our planet's fertility (it's the color of chlorophyll) as well as life itself

Blue: Healing, peace, psychism, patience, happiness. Blue is the color of the element of water. Symbolic of the ocean, sleep, twilight, and the sky. The Zuni employed this color to represent the west

Purple: Power, healing severe disease, spirituality, meditation, religion. Purple was once a European symbol of royalty; today it symbolizes the divine

White: Protection, purification, all purposes. Symbolic of the moon, freshness, snow, cold, and potential. Because white contains all colors, it can be utilized for every magical purpose. White symbolized the east to the Zuni

Black: Banishing negativity, absorbing negativity. Symbolizes outer space and the universe. Black is the absence of colors. In some cultures, black represented fertility (as in quite fruitful black earth); in others, wisdom. In our culture it has been curiously linked with evil, due to religious associations. It is not an evil color

Brown: Used for spells involving animals, usually in combination with other colors. Brown also represents soil and, to a lesser degree, fertility of the earth

Shells

Shells can be found on beaches throughout the world. The following list is rather short, due to the great variety of shells. For best results, use shells that have washed up on beaches; those commercially available may have been harvested, their inhabitants killed, and then sold. These shells are of lesser value in magic and those that use them may wish to say a rite of release for the shell's creators.

The colors of the shells can be kept in mind when determining their magical uses.

Abalone: General use. Use to contain empowered herbs, stones, and other magical objects

Clam shells: Used for purification and love. A small clam shell may be etched with a rune and made into a potent talisman

Conches: Love magic

Cone shells: Used in protective spell crafts

Cowries: Cowries are specific tools of prosperity and money; many cultures once used them as money. Some contemporary religions associate cowries with goddesses and with female mysteries. In this respect, they're fine for enhancing spirituality

Left-handed whelks: Use for making dramatic, positive changes in your life

Limpets: Courage, confidence, physical strength

Moon shells: Psychic awareness, purification, and peace

Olive shells: Healing

Oysters: Love and good fortune

Tooth (dentalium) shells: Money

Sand dollars: Wisdom

Scallops: Useful for spells involving travel and movement

Herbs

Many of these herbs are readily available in any food market. Sources of others can be found in the appendix.

Courage: Columbine, mullein, thyme, tonka, yarrow

Friendship: Lemon, passion flower, sweetpea

Happiness: Catnip, celandine, hyacinth, lavender, marjoram, meadowsweet, purslane, saffron, St. John's wort

Healing: Allspice, angelica, apple, carnation, cedar, cinnamon, elder, eucalyptus, fennel, gardenia, lemon balm, peppermint, sandalwood, vervain, willow

Love: Aster, basil, cardamom, catnip, camomile, clove, coriander, dragon's blood, ginger, juniper, lavender, lemon verbena, orris, rose, rosemary

Money: Alfalfa, almond, cinnamon, clove, corn, ginger, heliotrope, honeysuckle, mace, marjoram, nutmeg, orange bergamot, poppy, sassafras, sesame, vetivert, woodruff

Protection: Anise, bay, calamus, caraway, chrysanthemum, clover, dill, elder, fennel, frankincense, garlic, mistletoe, myrrh, parsley, pepper, pine, rosemary, Spanish moss

Psychic awareness: Acacia, borage, citron, flax, galangal, lemongrass, mace, mugwort, rose, star anise, yarrow, sumbul, thyme, yarrow, yerba santa

Purification: Anise, bay, benzoin, broom, cedar, copal, hyssop, lavender, lemon, lemon verbena, peppermint, pepper tree, rosemary, turmeric, vervain

Spirituality: Frankincense, gardenia, gum arabic, myrrh, sandalwood, sweet grass, wood aloe

Stones

Stones are powerful additions to spells and rites. Here are some of the most famous together with their magical powers.

Courage: Garnet, quartz crystal

Friendship: Amethyst, chrysocolla, rose quartz

Happiness: Amethyst, chrysoprase

Healing: Carnelian, hematite, jade, peridot

Love: Amethyst, rose quartz

Money: Aventurine, bloodstone, jade, tiger's-eye

Protection: Carnelian, garnet, lava, quartz crystal

Psychic awareness: Aquamarine, lapis lazuli

Purification: Aquamarine, calcite

Sprituality: Calcite, lepidolite, sugilite

Feathers

The magical qualities of feathers are determined by their color (and, sometimes, by the birds from which they fell). Below is a composite of feather lore from (mostly) European folk magic sources, and it differs from that of color symbolism in general.

It's always best to use found feathers as opposed to purchased feathers. Walks in parks, or in zoos, can provide a wealth of materials. If you keep birds, you have an even more reliable supply. Never harm a bird to obtain a feather.

White: Purification, spirituality, hope, protection, peace, blessings of the moon

Green: Money, fertility, growth

Brown: Health, stability, grounding, the home

Orange: Attraction, energy success

Yellow: Intelligence, blessings of the sun

Red: Courage, good fortune, life

Pink: Love

Gray: Peace, neutrality

Blue: Psychic awareness, peace, health

Black feathers: Not recommended

Red and brown: Healing animals

Brown and white: Happiness

Gray and white: Hope, balance

Black and white: Union, protection

Green and red: Finances

Blue, white, and black: Change

Black and purple: Deep spirituality

Woods

This list can be consulted when crafting altars, magic wands, and other spell craft tools created from wood.

Balsa: Psychic awareness

Cedar: Healing, purification, protection

Cherry: Love

Ebony: Protection, magical energy

Elder: Spirituality, protection

Eucalyptus: Healing

Maple: Love, money

Oak: Strength, health

Pine: Money, healing, exorcism

Walnut: Health

APPENDIX

Mail-Order Sources
of Craft Supplies

THOUGH MANY ITEMS necessary for completion of the projects are free (feathers, wood, shells), others must be purchased. If you have no craft supply stores in your area, fear not—many supplies are available by mail. Addresses and catalog ordering information were correct when this manuscript was written.

At times, the search for the required materials presents the greatest challenge. If this occurs, keep in mind that you're on a quest: a quest for the raw ingredients of magic.

Such quests have long been a part of magic. Four hundred years ago, they often involved obtaining such elusive substances as serpent's eggs, mandrake roots, May dew, fern seed, and mad stones. Today, though the object of our quests may be as prosaic as a bag full of shells or sixteen green one-inch tiles, such objects may still elude us.

The quest for the raw materials of spell craft may be seen as a test of the magician's willingness to search and discover, and, most importantly, of the magician's patience. All of these objects can be obtained somewhere. If you continue to have difficulty, perform a ritual in which you empower a green candle (to represent physical objects) with a visualization of the objects coming into your life. Burn the candle for nine minutes each day. You will find them.

Herbs

Aphrodisia
282 Bleeker Street
New York NY 10018
A wide selection of dried herbs. Send $2.00 for catalog.

Eye of the Cat
3314 E. Broadway
Long Beach CA 90803
A wide selection of herbs. Send $8.00 for catalog.

San Francisco Herb Co.
250 14th Street
San Francisco CA 94103
Dried flowers, herbs and spices for potpourri.

Beads and Beading Supplies

Promenade's Le Bead Shop
PO Box 2092
Boulder CO 80306
Beads. Send $2.50 for full-color catalog.

Jewelry Supplies 4 Less
13001J Las Vegas Blvd. South
Las Vegas NV 89124
Beads, beading books and beading needles. Send $4.00 for catalog.

Zimmerman's
28844 34th St. N.
St. Petersburg FL 33713
Beads, paint and sewing supplies. Send $2.00 for catalog.

Essential Oils

Co-op Essentials
5364 Ehrlich Road, Suite 402
Tampa FL 33625
True essential oils. Send for price list.

Ledet Aromatic Oils
PO Box 2354
Fair Oaks CA 95628
True essential oils. Send $1.50 for price list.

Lifetree Aromatix
3949 Longridge Avenue
Sherman Oaks CA 91423
True essential oils. Send $1.75 for price list.

Candlemaking Supplies

Candlechem
PO Box 705
Randolph MA 02268
Candle dyes, wax additives, bees wax, genuine bayberry wax, and other needed items. Send $2.00 for catalog.

Wheat Weaving Supplies

Doxie Keller Enterprises
127 West 30th
Hutchinson KS 67502
Dried wheat, wheat weaving instruction books, wheat weaving instructional video tape. Send for brochure.

Quill-it
PO Box 1304
Elmhurst IL 60126
Dried wheat and wheat weaving books. Send $1.00 for catalog.

GLOSSARY

Amulet: A magically empowered object that deflects specific (usually negative) energies. It may be carried, worn, or put in a specific place. Compare with **talisman**.

Bane: That which destroys life; is unuseful, poisonous, destructive or evil.

Baneful: See bane.

B.C.E.: Before Common Era; the nonreligious equivalent of B.C.

Blessing: The act of conferring positive energy upon a person, place, or thing. It is usually a spiritual or religious practice.

C.E.: Common Era; the nonreligious equivalent of A.D.

Charging: See **empowering**.

Charm: A magically empowered object carried to attract positive energies.

Clockwise: The traditional form of movement in positive magic. (If you're standing facing a tree, move to your left and walk in a circle around it. That's clockwise motion.) Also known as deosil movement.

Conscious mind: The analytical, materially based, rational half of our consciousness. Compare with **psychic mind.**

Craft: An art, especially that made with the hands. See also **spell craft.**

Cursing: The deliberate (and rare) movement of negative energies to affect a person, place, or thing.

Deosil: See **clockwise.**

Divination: The magical art of discovering the unknown by interpreting random patterns or symbols. Sometimes incorrectly referred to as "fortunetelling."

Elements, the: Earth, air, fire, and water. These four essences are the building blocks of the universe, and ancient magical sources of **energy.** In magic, earth energy is associated with the north; with the color green, with money, and stability. Air energy is associated with the east; with yellow, with travel, and the intellect. Fire is associated with the south; with red, with protection, and with sex. Water is associated with the west; with blue, with love, and with psychic awareness. The energy of the elements is often used in magic.

Empowering: The act of moving **energy** into an object.

Energy: A general term for the currently unmeasureable (but real) power that exists within all natural objects and beings—including our own bodies. It is used in **folk magic.** See also **personal power.**

Folk magic: The practice of magic utilizing **personal power,** in conjunction with natural tools, in a nonreligious framework, to cause positive change.

Herb: Any plant used in magic.

"Luck, good": An individual's ability to make timely, correct decisions, to perform correct actions and to place herself or himself in positive situations. "Bad luck" stems from ignorance and an unwillingness to accept self-responsibility.

Magic: The movement of natural (yet subtle) **energies** to manifest positive, needed change. Magic is the process of "rousing" energy, giving it purpose (through **visualization**), and releasing it to create a change. This is a natural (not supernatural) practice.

Meditation: Reflection, contemplation, turning inward toward the self or outward toward deity or nature.

Pagan: From the Latin *paqanus*, a "country dweller" or "villager." Today it's used as a general term for followers of **Wicca** and other polytheistic, magic-embracing religions. Pagans aren't Satanists, dangerous, or evil.

Pentagram: An interlaced five-pointed star (one point at its top) that has been used for thousands of years as a protective device. Today the pentagram is also associated with the **element** of earth and with **Wicca.** It has no evil associations.

Personal power: That energy which sustains our bodies. We first absorb it from our biological mothers within the womb and, later, from food, water, the moon and sun, and other natural objects. We release personal power during stress, exercise, sex, conception, and childbirth. **Magic** is usually a movement of personal power for a specific goal.

Power: See **energy; personal power.**

Projective hand: The talented hand; that with which we write, used in magic as a channel of **personal power.** Compare with **receptive hand.**

Psychic awareness: The act of being consciously psychic, in which the **psychic mind** and the **conscious mind** are linked and working in harmony.

Psychic mind: The subconscious or unconscious mind, in which we receive psychic impulses. The psychic mind is at work when we sleep, dream, and meditate.

Receptive hand: The hand that we do not write with. In magic, the hand through which power is drawn into the human body. Compare with **projective hand.**

Rite: See **ritual.**

Ritual: Ceremony. A specific form of movement, manipulation of objects, or inner processes designed to produce desired effects. In **magic** it allows the magician to move energy toward needed goals. A **spell** is a magical rite.

Runes: Stick-like figures, some of which are remnants of old Teutonic alphabets; others are pictographs. These symbols are once again being widely used in all forms of **magic.**

Spell: The mainstay of **folk magic,** spells are simply magical rites. They're usually nonreligious and often include spoken words.

Spell craft: Within the parameters of this book, it consists of the ritual creation of, and use of, specialized magical objects.

Talisman: An object ritually **charged** with power to attract a specific force or energy to its bearer. Compare with **amulet.**

Visualization: The process of forming mental images. Magical visualization consists of forming images of needed goals during **magic**. It's a function of the **conscious mind**.

Widdershins: Counterclockwise ritual motion, usually avoided in **folk magic**.

Wicca: A contemporary **Pagan** religion with spiritual roots in the earliest expressions of reverence of nature as a manifestation of the divine. Wicca views deity as Goddess and God; thus it is polytheistic. It also embraces the practice of **magic** and accepts reincarnation. Religious festivals are held in observance of the Full Moon and other astronomical (and agricultural) phenomena. It has no association with Satanism.

Wiccan: Of or relating to **Wicca**.

Witch: Anciently, a European practitioner of pre-Christian **folk magic** particularly that relating to herbs, healing, wells, rivers, and stones. One who practiced **Witchcraft**. Later, this term's meaning was deliberately altered to denote demented, dangerous beings who practiced destructive magic and who threatened Christianity. This latter definition is false. (Some **Wiccans** also use the word to describe themselves.)

Witchcraft: The craft of the Witch. Magic, especially magic utilizing personal power in conjunction with the energies within stones, herbs, colors, and other natural objects. While this does have spiritual overtones, Witchcraft, according to this definition, isn't a religion. However, some followers of **Wicca** use this word to denote their religion.

BIBLIOGRAPHY

Agar, Catherine, Diethold Buchheim, et. al. *The Beautiful Naturecraft Book*. New York: Sterling, 1979. (This British book contains a ten-page section on wheat weaving, with color photographs and step-by-step instructions.)

Arvoirs, Edmond. *Making Mosaics*. Lanham, Md.: Littlefield, Adams and Co., 1964. (The history of mosaics.)

Baity, Elizabeth Chesley. *Man Is a Weaver*. New York: The Viking Press, 1942. (The history of spinning.)

Berrin, Kathleen, editor. *Art of the Huichol Indians*. San Francisco/New York: The Fine Arts museum of San Francisco/Harry N. Abrams, Inc., 1978. (Enthralling account of Huichol sacred art, including shaman's arrows, god's eyes, and much more. Beautiful photographs.)

Bird, Adren J., and Josephine Puninani Kanekoa Bird. *Hawaiian Flower Lei Making*. Honolulu: University of Hawaii Press, 1987. (Step-by-step instructions for creating a wide variety of leis [floral garlands]. An excellent introduction.)

Budge, E. A. Wallis. *Amulets and Talismans*. New Hyde Park, N.Y.: University Books, 1968. (Magical lore regarding hands.)

Cavendish, Richard, editor. *An Illustrated Encyclopedia of Mythology*. New York: Crescent Books, 1984. (Deities connected with crafts.)

Dooling, D. M., editor. *A Way of Working: The Spiritual Dimension of Craft*. New York: Parabola Books, 1986. (The introduction to this book is filled with insight into the nonphysical nature of craft; the rest of the book is quite difficult, as the essays are marred by sexism and a truly remarkable Christian bias that seems inappropriate.)

Eichler, Lillian. *The Customs of Mankind*. Garden City, N.Y.: Nelson Doubleday, 1924. (Information regarding the magical significance of hands.)

Ely, Evelyn. *Ojos De Dios*. Reprinted from *El Palacio*, Volume 77, No. 3. Santa Fe: The Museum of New Mexico, 1972. (An excellent introduction to the spiritual meanings and uses of god's eyes.)

Erlandsen, Ida-Merete, and Hetty Mooi. *The Bead Book*. New York: Van Nostrad, 1974. (The history and lore of beads.)

Frazer, James. *The Golden Bough*. New York: Macmillan, 1951. (Background information on the history of various handicrafts.)

Gandee, Lee R. *Strange Experience: The Secrets of a Hexenmeister*. Englewood Cliffs, N.J.: Prentice-Hall, 1971. (A curious, intimately personal book. Much lore and speculation regarding hex signs. Interesting reading.)

Grose, David. "The Formation of the Roman Glass Industry" in *Archaeology*. Volume 26, Number 4, July/August 1983. (A fine account of early glass workings.)

Hererra, J. E. *Hexology: The Art and Meaning of the Pennsylvania Dutch Hex Signs*. Gettysburg, Pa.: Dutchcraft Company, 1964. (Folk uses of and one interpretation of these symbols.)

Hochberg, Bette. *Handspindles*. Santa Cruz, Calif.: Bette and Bernard Hochberg, 1979. (An indepth, fully illustrated look at the history of hand spinning.)

——*Spin-Span-Spun*. Santa Cruz, Calif.: Bette and Bernard Hochberg, 1979. (A delightful collection of spinning lore, legend, and mythology.)

Howells, William. *Back of History*. New York: Doubleday, Anchor, 1963. (Clay in antiquity.)

Jayne, Walter Addison. *The Healing Gods of Ancient Civilizations*. 1925. Reprint. New Hyde Park, N.Y.: University Books, 1962. (Deities connected with crafts.)

Johnson, Doris, and Alec Coker. *The Complete Book of Straw Craft and Corn Dollies*. New York: Dover, 1987. (A remarkably detailed guide to this art. Dozens of photographs.)

Johnson, Mary Elizabeth, and Katherine Pearson. *Naturecraft*. Birmingham, Ala.: Oxmoor House, 1980. (A chapter of wheat weaving contains many projects. Also includes information on weaving and on the construction of looms.)

Katlyn. *Ocean Amulets*. Long Beach, Calif.: Mermade Magickal Arts, 1988. (A poetic guide to the magic of shells and of the sea.)

Klenke, William W. *Candlemaking*. Peoria, Ill.: The Manual Arts Press, 1946. (An early, exacting account of candle production.)

Koch, Rudolf. *The Book of Signs*. New York: Dover, 1955. (Runes and symbols.)

Lambeth, M. *Discovering Corn Dollies*. Aylesbury, England: Shire Publications Ltd., 1982. (A short, informative introduction to corn dollies and the art of wheat plaiting. Many illustrations and photographs but few practical instructions.)

Lippard, Lucy R. *Overlay: Contemporary Art and the Art of Pre-history.* New York: Pantheon, 1983. (A fascinating book, filled with photographs of both ancient and modern art. The text describes the mystical processes at work during the creation of art.)

Lippman, Deborah, and Paul Colin. *How to Make Amulets Charms and Talismans: What They Mean and How to Use Them.* New York: M. Evans and Co., 1974. (Interesting book of heavy-duty crafts, suffused with early '70s American-style folk magic. The stuffed vulture toy for children is a delight.)

Maringer, Johannes. *The Gods of Prehistoric Man.* Edited and translated from the German by Mary Ilford. New York: Alfred A. Knopf, 1960. (Handicrafts and speculation regarding their religious and magical meanings among prehistoric peoples. And yes, we're not fond of the sexist title.)

Merrifield, Ralph. *The Archaeology of Ritual and Magic.* New York: New Amsterdam Books, 1988. (An engrossing look at ritual archaeological remains, primarily in England. A fine section on Witch bottles.)

Pennick, Nigel. *Skulls, Cats and Witch Bottles: The Ancient Art of House Protection.* Cambridge, England: Nigel Pennick Editions, 1986. (Fascinating historic information regarding Witch bottles in England.)

Pepper, Elizabeth, and John Wilcox. *Witches All: A Treasury From Past Editions of the Witches' Almanac.* New York: Grosset and Dunlap, 1977. (The magical lore of feathers.)

Pittaway, Andy, and Bernard Scofeld. *Traditional English Country Crafts.* New York: Pantheon, 1975. (Though this book gives us complete details on such subjects as raising goats and beekeeping, those chapters outlining candle-making and wheat weaving are more closely attuned with our subject.)

Potts, Albert M. *The World's Eye*. Lexington, Ky.: The University Press of Kentucky, 1982. (An engrossing, multicultural investigation of both the good and the evil eye. Includes a chapter on god's eyes.)

Redfield, Robert. *The Folk Culture of Yucatan*. Chicago: The University of Chicago Press, 1941. (Corn myths and magic.)

Smith, Elmer L. *Hex Signs and Other Barn Decorations*. Lebanon, Pa.: Applied Arts Publishers, 1986. (A fascinating, footnoted excursion into these familiar symbols. One of the best. Photographs and illustrations throughout.)

Starhawk. *The Spiral Dance*. San Francisco: Harper & Row, 1979. (Deities of crafts.)

Tanner, June. *Let's Make a Mosaic*. New York: Franklin Watts, 1968. (Mosaic techniques.)

Thomas, Diane. *The Handcrafter's Creative Ojo Book*. Phoenix: Hunter, 1976. (Making your own.)

Thompson, C. J. S. *The Hand of Destiny: Folklore and Superstition for Everyday Life*. New York: Bell, 1989. (Chapter 6 discusses "The Folk-Lore of the Hand." An intriguing book.)

Toor, Frances. *A Treasury of Mexican Folkways*. New York: Crown, 1973. (Extensive Huichol information.)

Tyson, Donald. *Rune Magic*. St. Paul, Minn.: Llewellyn Publications, 1988. (Information concerning the magical uses of runes.)

Zook, Jacob, and Jane Zook. *Hexology: The History and Meaning of the Hex Symbols*. Paradise, Pa.: Jacob Zook, n.d. (Yet another interpretation of these symbols, with full color photographs.)

☽ REACH FOR THE MOON

Llewellyn publishes hundreds of books on your favorite subjects! To get these exciting books, including the ones on the following pages, check your local bookstore or order them directly from Llewellyn.

Order by Phone
- Call toll-free within the U.S. and Canada, 1-877-NEW-WRLD
- In Minnesota, call (651) 291-1970
- We accept VISA, MasterCard, and American Express

Order by Mail
- Send the full price of your order (MN residents add 7% sales tax) in U.S. funds, plus postage & handling to:
  Llewellyn Worldwide
  P.O. Box 64383, Dept. 0-87542-185-7
  St. Paul, MN 55164–0383, U.S.A.

Postage & Handling
- **Standard** (U.S., Mexico, & Canada)

If your order is:
  $20 or under, add $5
  $20.01–$100, add $6
  Over $100, shipping is free

(Continental U.S. orders ship UPS. AK, HI, PR, & P.O. Boxes ship USPS 1st class. Mex. & Can. ship PMB.)

- **Second Day Air** (Continental U.S. only): $10 for one book plus $1 per each additional book
- **Express** (AK, HI, & PR only) [Not available for P.O. Box delivery. For street address delivery only.]: $15 for one book plus $1 per each additional book
- **International Surface Mail:** $20 or under, add $5 plus $1 per item; $20.01 and over, add $6 plus $1 per item
- **International Airmail:** Books—Add the retail price of each item; Non-book items—Add $5 per item

Please allow 4–6 weeks for delivery on all orders.
Postage and handling rates subject to change.

Discounts
We offer a 20% discount to group leaders or agents. You must order a minimum of 5 copies of the same book to get our special quantity price.

FREE CATALOG

Get a free copy of our color catalog, *New Worlds of Mind and Spirit*. Subscribe for just $10.00 in the United States and Canada ($30.00 overseas, airmail). Call 1-877-NEW-WRLD today!

Visit our website at www.llewellyn.com for more information.

The Magical Household

SCOTT CUNNINGHAM &
DAVID HARRINGTON

Whether your home is a small apartment or a palatial mansion, you want it to be something special. Now it can be with *The Magical Household*. Learn how to make your home more than just a place to live. Turn it into a place of security, life, fun, and magic. Here you will not find the complex magic of the ceremonial magician. Rather, you will learn simple, quick, and effective magical spells that use nothing more than common items in your house: furniture, windows, doors, carpet, pets, etc. You will learn to take advantage of the intrinsic power and energy that is already in your home, waiting to be tapped. You will learn to make magic a part of your life. The result is a home that is safeguarded from harm and a place that will bring you happiness, health, and more.

0-87542-124-5
208 pp., 5¼ x 8, illus. $9.95

Also Available in Spanish

The Complete Book of Incense, Oils & Brews

SCOTT CUNNINGHAM

For centuries the composition of incenses, the blending of oils, and the mixing of herbs have been used by people to create positive changes in their lives. With this book, the curtains of secrecy have been drawn back, providing you with practical, easy-to-understand information that will allow you to practice these methods of magical cookery.

Scott Cunningham, world-famous expert on magical herbalism, first published *The Magic of Incense, Oils and Brews* in 1986. *The Complete Book of Incense, Oils and Brews* is a revised and expanded version of that book. Scott took readers' suggestions from the first edition and added more than 100 new formulas. Every page has been clarified and rewritten, and new chapters have been added.

There is no special, costly equipment to buy, and ingredients are usually easy to find. The book includes detailed information on a wide variety of herbs, sources for purchasing ingredients, substitutions for hard-to-find herbs, a glossary, and a chapter on creating your own magical recipes.

0-87542-128-8
288 pp., 6 x 9, illus. $14.95

Also Available in Spanish

Cunningham's Encyclopedia of Magical Herbs
SCOTT CUNNINGHAM

This is the most comprehensive source of herbal data for magical uses ever printed! Almost every one of the over 400 herbs are illustrated, making this a great source for herb identification. For each herb you will also find: magical properties, planetary rulerships, genders, associated deities, folk and Latin names, and much more. To make this book even easier to use, it contains a folk name cross-reference, and all of the herbs are fully indexed. There is also a large annotated bibliography, and a list of mail-order suppliers so you can find the books and herbs you need. Like all of Cunningham's books, this one does not require you to use complicated rituals or expensive magical paraphernalia. Instead, it shares with you the intrinsic powers of the herbs. Thus, you will be able to discover which herbs, by their very nature, can be used for luck, love, success, money, divination, astral projection, safety, psychic self-defense, and much more. Besides being interesting and educational it is also fun, and fully illustrated with unusual woodcuts from old herbals. This book has rapidly become the classic in its field. It enhances books such as 777 and is a must for all Wiccans.

0-87542-122-9
336 pp., 6 x 9, illus.   **$14.95**
Also Available in Spanish